THE HOLOCAUST

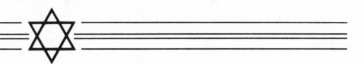

Selected Documents in Eighteen Volumes

John Mendelsohn
EDITOR

Donald S. Detwiler
ADVISORY EDITOR

A GARLAND SERIES

CONTENTS OF THE SERIES

THE HOLOCAUST

6. Jewish Emigration 1938–1940
Rublee Negotiations
and the Intergovernmental Committee

Introduction by
John Mendelsohn

GARLAND PUBLISHING, INC.
NEW YORK • LONDON
1982

These documents have been reproduced from copies in
the National Archives. Dr. Mendelsohn's work was carried out entirely on his own time and without endorsement or official participation by the National Archives as
an agency.

Library of Congress Cataloging in Publication Data
Main entry under title:

Jewish emigration 1938–1940, Rublee negotiations,
and Intergovernmental Committee.

(The Holocaust ; 6)
1. Jews—Germany—Migrations—Sources.
2. Germany—Emigration and immigration—Sources.
3. Rublee, George, 1868–
I. Intergovernmental Committee on Refugees.   II. Series.
D810.J4H655   vol. 6   940.53′15′03924s   81-80314
[DS135.G33]   [940.53′15′03924]   AACR2
ISBN 0-8240-4880-6

Design by Jonathan Billing

The volumes in this series have been printed on
acid-free, 250-year-life paper.

Printed in the United States of America

ACKNOWLEDGMENTS

I owe a debt of gratitude to many people who aided me during various stages of preparing these eighteen volumes. Of these I would like to mention by name a few without whose generous efforts this publication would have been impossible. I would like to thank Donald B. Schewe of the Franklin D. Roosevelt Library in Hyde Park, New York, for his speedy and effective help. Sally Marcks and Richard Gould of the Diplomatic Branch of the National Archives in Washington, D.C., extended help beyond their normal archival duties, as did Timothy Mulligan and George Wagner from the Modern Military Branch. Edward J. McCarter in the Still Picture Branch helped a great deal. I would also like to thank my wife, Tish, for letting me spend my evenings during the past few years with these volumes rather than with her and our children, Michael and Lisa.

J. M.

INTRODUCTION

It is rarely an easy decision to leave one's home country, and often people will do so only under intense pressure. This was clearly the case for the Jews who had not left Germany during the first few years of the Nazi regime. Some of the younger Jews, particularly those who had matured during the thirties, were by 1938 more willing to go than their elders. Others, young and old, could not bring themselves to leave and speculated against all odds that they could survive the Nazis as their ancestors before them had survived persecution. Who could have foreseen that the Nazi solution to the "Jewish question" was extermination, not only for Germany's Jews, but also for those living in other parts of Europe that were accessible to Nazi power?

Despite the reluctance of some of the Jews to leave, a much larger number attempted to emigrate than were able to obtain visas and gain entry into the often reluctant receiving countries. Although less was done than might have been to relieve the suffering of the persecuted Jews, the outside world did not stand idly by watching the Nazis heap indignities and disabilities upon the Jews in Germany. A group of Jewish families in the United States, for example, collected sufficient funds to effect the emigration of fifty Jewish children from Germany. The children were comfortably accommodated on an estate in Philadelphia, where they were introduced to the American way of life while awaiting the arrival of their parents who were to emigrate at a later time. A larger group of children emigrated from Vienna to a safe haven in England under similar conditions.

In addition to attempts by individuals or groups to relieve the suffering of the Jews in Germany and Austria, national and international activities brought about some further relief. One of the positive results of the conference at Evian-les-Bains held in the summer of 1938 to deal with the refugee problem was the establishment of an intergovernmental committee on refugees. George Rublee, a veteran trouble-shooter, negotiator, and official of the Department of State, headed the intergovernmental committee and conducted negotiations with Hjalmar Schacht, president of the *Reichsbank*. Following Schacht's dismissal these negotiations were continued by Helmuth Wohlthat, a foreign exchange and currency expert. After difficult negotiations an agreement was reached that enabled a number of Jews to leave Germany, but the outbreak of the Second World War in September 1939 severely curtailed further

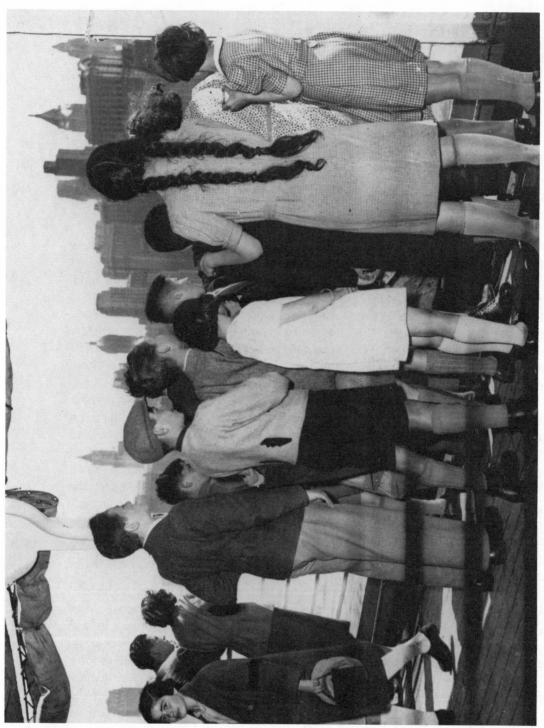

Jewish refugee children on the deck of the S.S. *President Harding* with the lower New York skyline in the background. They were among fifty privately sponsored Jewish children on their way to an estate in Philadelphia where they were to await the arrival of their parents. June 3, 1939.
National Archives and Records Service 306-NT-648E-9

emigration. Nonetheless, emigration of Jews continued through various routes until the entry of the Soviet Union into the war in the summer of 1941. Whatever emigration still continued was slowed to an insignificant trickle with the attack on Pearl Harbor, which brought the United States into the war. Thereafter emigration was restricted to individual cases largely in the Balkans and Turkey. In all, though, about half a million Jews left Germany, Austria, and Bohemia-Moravia. Some went only as far as Holland, Belgium, or France, where the Nazi killing machine eventually caught up with many of them. Thus the actual number of Jews saved by emigration was smaller than it appeared to be.

The documents reproduced in this volume originated in four record collections: the Nuernberg Trials prosecution document series; captured German records, particularly those of the German foreign ministry, the Reich leader of the SS, and the chief of the German police; the central decimal file of the records of the Department of State; and the papers of Myron C. Taylor, the chief of the American delegation to the Evian conference, which are now housed at the Franklin D. Roosevelt Library in Hyde Park, New York.

The documents pertain foremost to the negotiations by George Rublee with Hjalmar Schacht and Helmuth Wohlthat and to the work of the Intergovernmental Committee on Refugees. They also include documentation of the willingness of the Nazi authorities to release concentration camp inmates provided that visas were obtained for them and that means were available to pay an emigration levy of one thousand Reichsmark imposed by the Reich Association of Jews on emigrants. Other documents concern emigration regulations in Germany and reports on counterfeit landing permits and papers.

John Mendelsohn

SOURCE ABBREVIATIONS
AND DESCRIPTIONS

Nuernberg Document   Records from five of the twenty-five Nuernberg Trials
prosecution document series: the NG (Nuernberg
Government) series, the NI (Nuernberg Industrialist)
series, the NO (Nuernberg Organizations) series, the
NOKW (Nuernberg Armed Forces High Command)
series, and the PS (Paris-Storey) series. Also included
are such Nuernberg Trials prosecution records as
interviews, interrogations, and affidavits, excerpts
from the transcripts of the proceedings, briefs,
judgments, and sentences. These records were used by
the prosecution staff of the International Military
Tribunal at Nuernberg or the twelve United States
military tribunals there, and they are part of National
Archives Record Group 238, National Archives
Collection of World War II War Crimes Records.

OSS   Reports by the Office of Strategic Services in National
Archives Record Group 226.

SEA   Staff Evidence Analysis: a description of documents
used by the Nuernberg prosecution staff. Although the
SEA's tended to describe only the evidentiary parts of
the documents in the summaries, they describe the
document title, date, and sources quite accurately.

State CDF   Central Decimal File: records of the Department of
State in National Archives Record Group 59, General
Records of the Department of State.

T 120   Microfilm Publication T 120: records of the German
foreign office received from the Department of State
in Record Group 242, National Archives Collection of
Foreign Records Seized, 1941–. The following
citation system is used for National Archives

Microfilm Publications: The Microfilm Publication number followed by a slash, the roll number followed by a slash, and the frame number(s). For example, Document 1 in Volume I: T 120/4638/K325518—K325538.

T 175

Microfilm Publication T 175: records of the Reich leader of the SS and of the chief of the German police in Record Group 242.

U.S. Army and U.S. Air Force

Records relating to the attempts to cause the U.S. Army Air Force to bomb the extermination facilities at Auschwitz and the railroad center at Kaschau leading to Auschwitz, which are part of a variety of records groups and collections in the National Archives. Included are records of the United States Strategic Bombing Survey (Record Group 243), records of the War Refugee Board (Record Group 220), records of the Joint Chiefs of Staff, and other Army record collections.

War Refugee Board

Records of the War Refugee Board, located at the Franklin D. Roosevelt Library in Hyde Park, New York. They are part of National Archives Record Group 220, Records of Temporary Committees, Commissions and Boards. Included in this category are the papers of Myron C. Taylor and Ira Hirschmann.

CONTENTS

18   Notes by Legation Counsellor Rademacher of the German
     foreign ministry pertaining to the refusal to supply
     documentation for the emigration of Jews from France.
     September 15 to 19, 1941. With SEA.
     Nuernberg Document NG 3107   251

Notes

1. *Document 1.* Myron C. Taylor was the chairman of the American delegation to the Evian conference and President Roosevelt's special emissary to the Holy See on refugee questions. George Rublee was the director of the Intergovernmental Committee on Refugees and conducted negotiations with officials of the German Reich on the emigration of Jews.

2. *Document 2.* Ernst Woermann held various positions in the German foreign ministry including chief of the political division; he held the rank of ambassador. He was tried by an American military tribunal at Nuernberg in the so-called ministries case and sentenced to seven years imprisonment.

3. *Document 3.* Ernst von Weizsäcker was state secretary in the German foreign ministry from 1938 to 1943, when he was appointed German ambassador to the Holy See. Despite his claims that he was a member of the anti-Nazi resistance in Germany, an American military tribunal sentenced him in the so-called ministries case to seven years imprisonment.

4. *Document 4.* Hans Fischboeck was a state secretary who served in various capacities in the Nazi government usually in the fields of commerce and finance. In 1938 he was minister of commerce in the Seyss-Inquart cabinet in Austria.

5. *Document 5.* Hjalmar Horace Greeley Schacht held various financial posts in the Nazi government until 1939, when he fell from power and was himself persecuted. Most important was his position as president of the Reichsbank from 1923 to 1930. Later he conducted negotiations with George Rublee. In 1946 the International Military Tribunal at Nuernberg acquitted him of all charges including war crimes and crimes against humanity.

6. *Document 9.* Reinhardt Heydrich was the dreaded chief of the SS Reich security main office and of the security police and the security service. He was also acting protector of Bohemia-Moravia when he was assassinated in June 1942.

7. *Document 15.* The telegrams are by Alexander Kirk, the chargé d'affaires ad interim at the American embassy in Berlin.

8. *Document 16.* Adolf Eichmann was the chief of Amt IV B 4 in the Reich security main office of the SS; he headed the Office for Jewish Affairs of Secret State Police. He was tried by an Israeli court in Jerusalem, sentenced to death, and executed in 1962.

9. *Document 17.* Walter Schellenberg was the chief of Amt VI, foreign intelligence, of the security main office of the SS. An American military tribunal sentenced him in the so-called ministries case to six years imprisonment.

INTERGOVERNMENTAL COMMITTEE

Director :
Mr. GEORGE RUBLEE.

1, CENTRAL BUILDINGS,

WESTMINSTER,

LONDON, S.W.1.

October 14, 1938.

Dear Myron:

I wish to acknowledge the receipt of your very excellent and most interesting letter of September 30; also your note of October 6 enclosing the Portugal survey, as well as the copies of your speech before the Council on Foreign Relations which you kindly sent us.

I liked your speech. It contained the information which enabled your audience to understand how the Intergovernmental Committee was formed and what its functions are from the Evian Conference and before until the present time. This was, I should think, precisely what your audience wanted and provided the ground for you to stress the importance and urgency of our problem, as well as the difficulties before us.

In your letter I was, of course, particularly interested in learning that the President is willing to direct a personal appeal to Hitler at the right moment. You referred also to the possibility that the Prime Minister may bring the question of refugees to the attention of Hitler in person. You mention that Mr. Welles would communicate with me about the willingness of the President to appeal to Hitler and that you assume that I would in turn communicate with Lord Winterton so that the timing of these efforts might be consistent. Mr. Welles, however, has not said anything to me about the proposed action of the President. I am also inclined to doubt whether the Prime Minister will take up the refugee matter with Hitler. I think I reported to you before that Winterton told us that no conferences between the British and German Governments relating to a general settlement will occur be-

Doc. 1

1

The Honorable
    Myron C. Taylor,
        71 Broadway,
            New York, New York.

fore December and I do not know that they will then
occur. Furthermore, it is my opinion that the Foreign
Office would oppose any introduction of the refugee
matter as one of the subjects to be treated in a general settlement. It, therefore, seems to be probable
that we shall have to try to follow our original plan
in regard to the approach to Germany.

Almost immediately after my letter to you of October 12th, a cable came from the Department for the
Ambassador and myself in which the Department expressed
the view that it was desirable for me to go to Germany as soon as possible and set forth the instructions
which they propose to give to Hugh Wilson in regard to
approaching the German authorities. The Department
wished to ascertain whether the British Government would
be willing to give similar instructions to Sir Nevile
Henderson. Mr. Kennedy, I learned, through Herschel
Johnson, declined to take up the matter with the Foreign Office. Herschel reported that he said that,
as Director, I was an International Officer and that
it was not the place of an American Ambassador to act
on my behalf. He thought that I should take the matter up with Lord Winterton and that if I had no success with him that he might then permit Herschel to go
to the Foreign Office, but even as to that, he would
have to consider at the time whether this would be
advisable. It seemed to me rather strange that the
American Ambassador would consider that it was the
duty of an International Officer to present the views
of the American Government to the British Government.
However, I went ahead and did as he wished.

Yesterday Pell and I had a conference with Winterton. On the subject of the instructions to be given
to the British Ambassador as requested by the State
Department, Winterton said that the matter was being
considered at the Foreign Office and when they had
reached a decision, they would instruct the British
Ambassador in Washington to confer with the State Department about it. We also discussed with Winterton
the statement of the British Government concerning
the contribution that Government could make in the

reception of involuntary emigrants from Germany. I
am enclosing a copy of the memorandum of the conversation which Pell made. Winterton's attitude was
almost wholly negative and I felt that it was necessary for me to express my disappointment quite frankly
and to say that the failure of the British Government
to undertake a more definite commitment added very
much to my difficulties in negotiating successfully
either with Germany or with the other countries of
final settlement. Pell's memorandum, of course, gives
only a summary of the conversation. I was rather more
explicit and insistent than the impression conveyed by
the memorandum. The talk, however, was entirely friendly on both sides. I thought that Winterton was impressed by what I said but felt that he had no authority to offer more than he had.

Last night we all went to the buffet dinner given
by Ambassador Kennedy for the American Committee in
London of which we were members. I sat at the Ambassador's table and had an opportunity to have a few
words with him at the end of the meal. I remarked
that he had told me that if I got into a "jam" he
would help me. "Well," I said, "I am in a 'jam' and
I wish you would help me." He assured me that he
would talk to Lord Halifax when Halifax came back on
Monday and that he would also talk to the Prime Minister. He said that he had had a talk with the German
Ambassador earlier in the day and that the German Ambassador had said that Hitler was not quite "right"
for this matter yet. The Ambassador said that he had
read all my cables to the Department and that he understood my situation. I was encouraged by his manner
and tone which were more reassuring than I expected
after Herschel's report to me a day or two ago.

We are much comforted by the thought of your continued interest and support.

With warm regards from us all,

Sincerely yours,

George Rublee

Enclosure.

P.S. We have just heard from the Foreign Office
that the British concur with the draft instructions
to Wilson but they will strengthen the leading paragraph in the sense that they will say that they
leave full discretion to Henderson in Berlin as to
the time and manner of my approach. This leaves our
position very much where it was before, and I depend
now to a very great extent on Hugh Wilson's initiative.

4

Telephone :—ABBEY 6077-78-79.

INTERGOVERNMENTAL COMMITTEE.

Director :
MR. GEORGE RUBLEE.

1, CENTRAL BUILDINGS,

WESTMINSTER,

LONDON, S.W.1.

November 7, 1938.

Dear Myron:

Since my letter to you of November 2nd, there have been no further developments with respect to the Transfer Plan.

Since that time, however, we have heard from Hugh Wilson that Goering and Funk are of the opinion that I should be received in Berlin and are preparing a memorandum on the subject to be submitted to Hitler within a short time. We also hear from Wilson that Ribbentrop is opposed to my being received. From high sources at the Foreign Office here, we hear that Goering is coming to England some time between November 20th and the middle of December. I imagine you have all this information through the Department but I want to be sure you are absolutely up to date.

I want to suggest for your consideration the following which I have not communicated to the Department. On the basis of what we know now, it is apparent that the Germans are finding it difficult to make up their minds whether or not to receive me. If we should get further information that the answer is likely to be unfavorable, or that a situation has arisen where further diplomatic steps on our part are advisable before a formal answer comes from the German Government, it is conceivable that a further effort by the President either alone or in conjunction with Mr. Chamberlain, as outlined in your letter to me of September 30, might be appropriate. I am not at all convinced that a situation will develop in such a way as to make such a step advisable, or that we will get

The Honorable
    Myron C. Taylor,
       71 Broadway,
          New York, New York.

5

sufficient information as to what is going on in Germany
to recommend that such step be taken. But I do not want
to leave any stone unturned and I would like your advice
as to the feasibility and desirability of such step should
it appear to us that a situation has arisen where it is
clear that the answer of the German Government as to
whether I will be received in Berlin will be unfavorable.
If we are once turned down I do not see that any appeal
by the President or Mr. Chamberlain to Hitler could be
effective.

    With warm regards,

              Yours ever,

              George Rublee

6

I enclose a copy of a letter I wrote today to Mr. Warren
for your information.

November 7, 1938

Dear Mr. Werren:

I want to thank you for your recent letters of October
27 and 28. Your letters are very helpful to me in keeping in
touch with what is going on in the United States. As you have
recently seen, and are in touch with Mr. Taylor, I imagine he has
told you that things are moving at the German end.

(1) Press Reports - The New York Herald Tribune article
and the Lowell Thomas broadcast to which you referred are, of course,
extremely unfortunate, and we are at a loss to know how these reports got into the Press, especially as they are not entirely true.
It is becoming more and more apparent, however, that the only way
to get anything from the Dominions is to have a direct approach
made to the local Governments, and we hope much from Mr. Taylor's
proposed trip to Canada in this connection.

I do not know if I told you that I saw Sir Wyndham
Deedes a couple of weeks ago, who is on his way to South Africa
with Norman Bentwich. I hope they will canvass the situation for
us there. If you have any suggestions as to how a direct approach
might be made to the Australian and New Zealand Governments, I
would appreciate them.

(2) The Sudeten Situation - I note your attempts to
harmonize the activity of President Butler's Committee and your
Advisory Committee. In this connection, I do not know whether
Mr. Taylor informed you about certain difficulties we have been
having with the British Government.

Some time ago Sir Neill Malcolm flew to Prague with
the Lord Mayor. So far as I could find out, he was able to do
very little. He has, however, been subjected to criticism in
League circles on the ground that he had no business going there,
since the League has not recognized the transfer of the Sudeten
areas to Germany. The British Government naturally feel pecu-
liar responsibility for the Czech refugee situation, and after
Sir Neill's trip, Lord Winterton circulated a memorandum to the
Governments participating in the work of the Intergovernmental
Committee. This memorandum said in effect that the transfer of

the Sudeten areas has led to an extension of the problem of involuntary emigration from Germany coming within the scope of the Intergovernmental Committee. It further stated that of the involuntary emigrants in the transferred areas, those who are of German origin are in precisely the same position as, and should be assimilated to, the other involuntary emigrants in Germany and Austria. It further stated that the Director would circulate to members of the Committee such particulars as he is able to obtain as to the number and type of involuntary emigrants who have been, or may be created by the transfer of the Sudeten areas, as well as the conditions in which these persons are able to emigrate.

In its original form submitted to me by Lord Winterton for my comment, the memorandum contained certain features which seemed undesirable, and which were eliminated. It originally contained language distinguishing between Jewish and other involuntary emigrants which, as you know, we have always carefully avoided. It also contained suggestions that the Director should make certain investigation of the Sudeten refugee situation. Knowing as we did that the British Government had called in Dominion representatives and representatives of Scandinavian and other countries in an attempt to get them to commit themselves to receiving Sudeten refugees, and that in fact, the British Government intends to discriminate in favor of these, as opposed to other German refugees, we felt that any suggestion of discrimination in the memorandum as between Jewish and Non-Jewish and between Sudeten and other German refugees was very objectionable. As you can see, it would make our task practically hopeless in South America and elsewhere if it became known that the British Government was discriminating in this way. For instance, we recently had a talk with Mr. Lobo of Brazil in which he stated that the way to get Jews into Brazil and other South American countries was to call them Non-Aryan Catholics, and in effect, what every country wants is the Non-Jewish element among the refugees. Accordingly, any suggestion of official discrimination along these lines would have been extremely unfortunate. I tell you the above story in case you did not know it, in the hope that it may help you in harmonizing the activity of President Butler's Committee with the Advisory Committee. To complete the story, Lord Winterton sent Sir Walter Layton, who is particularly concerned with the Czech situation, around to see me the other day, obviously in the hope of persuading me to send some representative to Prague. Our position is the refugees in the Sudeten areas, of German origin, coming within the scope of the activity of the Intergovernmental Committee.

- 3 -

(3) <u>Projects</u> - I am delighted to hear about the Committee being able to study the various projects which you and Jaretzki are attempting to develop. Nothing has happened in the way of setting up a corresponding Committee in London of which Mr. Warburg originally spoke to me.

(4) Within the last day or so we received a formal statement from the British Government in answer to the request at Evian. I will send copies to you and Mr. Taylor as soon as possible. This statement, judged along the lines of my report to Winterton, is completely unsatisfactory in that the British are unwilling to state numbers and have apparently made no real effort with the Colonies or the Dominions. I appreciate their difficulties in connection with approaching the Dominions, but you can see what they will try to do if they feel they really have to, as in the case of the Sudeten refugee problem described above. I am informed privately, however, through Otto Schiff, that Great Britain is taking refugees at a really extraordinary rate said to approximate 25,000 a year.

(5) I note with interest the suggestion of the Advisory Committee that I should discuss with the German Government the stabilization of the situation of involuntary emigrants pending emigration.

Sincerely yours,

9

George L. Warren, Esq.,
        President's Advisory Committee on
                Political Refugees,
        122 E. 22nd Street,
                New York City, N.Y.

OFFICE OF CHIEF OF COUNSEL
FOR WAR CRIMES
APO 696-A   U.S.ARMY

STAFF EVIDENCE ANALYSIS, Ministries Division.

By: Mark Schafer
Date: 24 April 1947.

Document number: NG-1525.

Title and/or general nature: Note by WOERMANN indicating the
                                         German Foreign Office was using
                                         delaying tactics to stall the
                                         Rublee discussions.

Form of Document: Typed copy.

Stamps and other endorsements: None.

Date: 21 October 1938.

Source: "3216 26 Judenfrage U.St.S.
                                          24 Nr.2,"
                                         now at: FO-SD, Building 32, MDT,
                                         Berlin,
                                         (OCC CST 1096).

PERSONS OF ORGANIZATIONS IMPLICATED:

WOERMANN
WEIZSAECKER
"Referat Deutschland".

TO BE FILED UNDER THESE REFERENCE HEADINGS:

NG-Foreign Office
NG-Political and Racial Persecution.

SUMMARY:

WOERMANN reports that the British chargé d'affaires had
requested once more in the name of his government that Mr.RUBLEE
be given the opportunity to come to Berlin and start discussions,
not only on the Jewish problem, but on the problem of German
refugees in general.

WOERMANN states that he had given the Britisher an answer
similar to the one which the Under State Secretary (WEIZSAECKER)
had given the British ambassador. "Further I asked him not to
come to me again with this matter in a few days already. We
would transmit the desire to the competent authorities, but it
was not to be expected that a decision would be reached immediately.

Distribution: WEIZSAECKER
WOERMANN
"Referat Deutschland".

— END —

Berlin, den 2. Oktober 1938.

Der Britische Geschäftsträger suchte mich
heute auf, um im Anschluß an den kürzlichen Schritt des britischen Botschafters bei dem Herrn Staatssekretär nochmals
im Auftrage seiner Regierung zu bitten, daß Mr. Rublee
Gelegenheit gegeben wird, nach Berlin zu kommen. Es handele
sich dabei nicht nur um das Judenproblem sondern um die
deutschen Flüchtlinge überhaupt. Herr Rublee, den er, der
Geschäftsträger, aus Mexiko persönlich gut kenne, sei ein
ausgezeichneter Mann, der sicher hier mit dem nötigen Takt
vorgehen werde. Ich habe Sir George Ogilvie Forbes ähnlich
geantwortet, wie kürzlich der Staatssekretär dem Botschafter
geantwortet hatte. Ferner habe ich ihn gebeten, nicht schon
in ein paar Tagen nochmals mit der Angelegenheit anzukommen.
Wir würden den Wunsch an die inneren Ressorts weitergeben.
Es sei aber nicht zu erwarten, daß nun eine Entscheidung
sofort falle. Sir George meinte, daß Rublee insofern in einer
unangenehmen Lage sei, als er seine Arbeiten im Übrigen
abgeschlossen habe und nun nicht weiter komme, ohne die
deutsche Stellungnahme zu kennen.

gez. Woermann

St.S.
Dg. Pol.
Pol. VII
Referat Deutschland
Pol. II

11

OFFICE OF CHIEF OF COUNSEL
FOR WAR CRIMES
APO 696-A   U.S.ARMY

STAFF EVIDENCE ANALYSIS, Ministries Division.

By: Mark Schafer.
Date: 24 April 1947.

Document number: NG-1524.

Title and/or general nature: Note signed by WEIZSAECKER indi-
                                cating delaying tactics used by
                                the German Foreign Office to stall
                                the Rublee-discussions on the
                                Jewish problem.

Form of Document: Original typescript.

Stamps and other endorsements: Hand-written signature of WEIZ_
                                saecker.

Date: 2 November 1938.

Source: "3216 26 Judenfrage U.St.S.
                                 24 Nr. 2,"
                                now at: FO-SD, Building 32 HDR,
                                Berlin,
                                (OCC IT 1095).

Doc. 3

12

PERSONS OR ORGANIZATIONS IMPLICATED:

                                WEIZSAECKER
                                WOERMANN.

TO BE FILED UNDER THESE REFERENCE HEADINGS:

                                NG-Foreign Office
                                NG-Political and Racial Persecution

SUMMARY:

    WEIZSAECKER writes the following note:
    "The American ambassador reminded me again to-day of the
visit of RUBLEE in Berlin. I have consoled him".

                    Distribution: WOERMANN
                                  "Referat Deutschland".

- END -

Berlin, den 2. November 1933.

Der Amerikanische Botschafter
erinnerte mich heute wieder an den Besuch R u b l e e 's
in Berlin. Ich habe ihn vertröstet.

[signature]

13

Herrn Unterstaatssekretär
  " Dg. Pol.
Referat Deutschland

OFFICE OF CHIEF OF COUNSEL
FOR WAR CRIMES
APO 696-A   U.S.ARMY

STAFF EVIDENCE ANALYSIS, Ministries Division.

By: Mark Schafer
Date: 24 April 1947.

Document number: NG-1523.

Title and/or general nature: Note by WOERMANN regarding the
                              discussions FISCHBOECK-RUBLEE
                              on the emigration of Jews.

Form of Document: Typed copy.

Stamps and other endorsements:
                              None.

Date: 16 November 1938.

Source: "3216 26 Judenfrage U.St.S.
                              24 Nr.2;"
                              now at: FO-SD, Building 32,
                              MD3, Berlin,
                              (OCC BBT 1091).

Doc. 4

14

PERSONS OR ORGANIZATIONS IMPLICATED:

                              WOERMANN
                              FISCHBOECK
                              STUCKART
                              ALBRECHT
                              SCHWERIN VON KROSIGK
                              SCHACHT.

TO BE FILED UNDER THESE REFERENCE HEADINGS:

                              NG-Foreign Office
                              NG-Political and Racial Perse-
                                 cution
                              NG-Ministry of Finance
                              NG-Ministry of Economics
                              NG-Ministry of Interior.

SUMMARY:

        WOERMANN reports that RIBBENTROP has agreed to a
"private" discussion between FISCHBOECK of Austria and RUBLEE
regarding the emigration of Jews.

        The Minister of Finance, the Minister of Economics and
Under State Secretary STUCKART have all agreed to the idea.

- END -

Berlin, den 16.November 1938.

        Der Herr Reichs-minister hat sich damit einverstanden er-
klärt, dass Minister Fischboeck entsprechend dem von ihm gemachten Vorschlag die Verbindung mit Herrn Rublee in der Frage der jüdischen Auswanderung aufnimmt. Die Zusammenkunft soll
jedoch in privater Form und weder in Berlin noch in London
stattfinden. Bevor ich diesen Auftrag an Minister Fischboeck
übermittele, müsste das Einverständnis der beteiligten Ressorts herbeigeholt werden. Nach Angabe von Minister Fischboeck
gemäss meiner früheren Aufzeichnung haben der Reichsfinanzmi-
nister, der Reichswirtschaftsminister und Staatssekretär
Stuckert bereits zugestimmt. Es wäre aber von diesen, wohl am
besten durch Schnellbrief, eine Zusage zu erreichen, ebenso
von der Gestapo. Ferner wäre wohl auch das Reichsbankdirektori-
um und der Stellvertreter des Führers zu beteiligen.

15

        Hiermit
                dem Referat Deutschland
        mit der Bitte um baldige weitere Veranlassung.

                        (gez.) Woermann

Durchdruck an
        Dir. W
        Dir.Recht
        Dg.Pol.

OFFICE OF CHIEF OF COUNSEL
FOR WAR CRIMES
APO 696-A   U.S.ARMY

STAFF EVIDENCE ANALYSIS, Ministries Division.

By: Mark Schefer.
Date: 23 April 1947.

Document number: NG-1521.

Title and/or general nature: Note by WEIZSAECKER, complaining
                                     that SCHACHT failed to secure the
                                     approval of the Foreign Office be-
                                     fore conducting the RUBLEE-dis-
                                     cussions in London.

Form of Document: Typed copy.

Stamps and other endorsements:
                                     Initialed WOERMANN (?)

Date: 20 December 1938.

Source: "3216 26 Judenfrage U.St.S.
                                     24 Nr.2; "
                                     now at: FO - SD, Building 32,
                                     MDB, Berlin,
                                     (OCC BDT 1089).

Doc. 5

16

PERSONS OR ORGANIZATIONS IMPLICATED:

                                     WEIZSAECKER
                                     WOERMANN
                                     ASCHMANN
                                     SCHACHT
                                     "Referat Deutschland".

TO BE FILED UNDER THESE REFERENCE HEADINGS:

                                     NG-Foreign Office
                                     NG-Political and Racial Per-
                                         secution.

SUMMARY:

        Referring to an article appearing in the Berliner Zeitung
on the SCHACHT discussions in London with regard to the Jewish
question, WEIZSAECKER heavily criticizes SCHACHT for having
failed to obtain authorization from RIBBENTROP before em-
barking for London. SCHACHT based his defense on a "direct
order by the Fuehrer" which is supposed to have given him
authority for the talks.

                    Distribution: WOERMANN
                                  ASCHMANN
                                  "Referat Deutschland".

- END -

Berlin, den 20. Dezember 1938

NG - 1521

Auf Grund der in der B.Z. vom 19. Dezember
erschienenen Notiz "Schachts Gespräche in London,
der Zweck der Reise" hat mich der Herr Reichsminister beauftragt, den Reichsbankpräsidenten Schacht
anzurufen, um ihn wegen dieses Artikels und insbesondere seines Schlußsatzes sowie wegen der Erörterung
der Materie in London zur Rede zu stellen. Ich führ-
te bei dem Telefongespräch mit Präsident Schacht u.a.
aus, der Herr Reichsminister habe sich über den betreffenden Artikel gewundert und zwar sowohl wegen der Ver-
öffentlichung selbst als auch wegen der Behandlung
einer solch grundsätzlichen Frage der auswärtigen Politik in London. Die Materie sei seit 6 Monaten zwischen
den ausländischen diplomatischen Vertretungen und dem
Auswärtigen Amt in Erörterung und von uns bisher ganz
negativ behandelt worden. Ich hätte zu fragen, ob etwa
ein Auftrag des Führers vorgelegen habe, die Materie
ohne Fühlungnahme mit dem Herrn Reichsaußenminister zu
erörtern. Die Konsequenz würde dann sein, daß der Präsident Schacht ja auch die weiteren Verhandlungen mit
den fremden Regierungen zu führen haben würde. Durch
den Schlußpassus des Zeitungsartikels werde die bisherige Linie des Reichsaußenministers desavouiert und
in der Frage für die Zukunft vorgegriffen.

Präsident Schacht gab unumwunden zu, daß der
Artikel von ihm stamme. Es handle sich um einen Auftrag des Führers, den er, der Präsident, in dem ihm
gesteckten Rahmen in London ausgeführt habe. Der Führer wünsche von ihm Berichterstattung nach Rückkehr.

Herrn Reichsminister   Sr.
  " Unterstaatssekretär
  " Dg. Pol.
  " Direktor W.
  " Gesandten Aschmann
Referat Deutschland

17

Dr. Schacht, habe sich daher jetzt beim Führer zum
Vortrag gemeldet, hoffe diesen in 1 - 2 Tagen erstatten
zu können und werde danach umgehend sich auch bei dem
Herrn Reichsminister zur Berichterstattung einfinden.
Ehe er dem Führer Meldung gemacht habe, möchte er sich
in der Sache nicht weiter äußern.

Im übrigen, so fuhr Präsident Schacht fort,
sei ihm durch Feldmarschall Göring gesagt worden, er
möge die Besprechungen, welche er geführt habe, in London aufnehmen. Göring und Schacht hätten die Materie
eingehend mit einander erörtert. Der Feldmarschall
wünsche die Sache aus dem Gebiete der Politik in das
rein wirtschaftliche hinüberzuspielen und habe dazu
nach seiner Äußerung auch vom Führer einen ausdrücklichen Auftrag. Über die Zuständigkeiten erklärte Schacht
in der Sache nicht mehr zu wissen, als was der Feldmarschall ihm gesagt habe. Er glaube also korrekt gehandelt zu haben und sei auch ganz bewußt in London allen
Erörterungen politischer Natur, um die prominente Engländer ihn gebeten hätten, aus dem Wege gegangen. Seine
Reise nach London gehe auf eine private Einladung von
Norman zurück. Es habe sich um Erörterungen von Bank
zu Bank gehandelt, wobei die Judenauswanderung ein
Nebenthema gebildet habe. Trotz der ausdrücklichen
Aufforderung durch den Feldmarschall habe Schacht jedoch auf dem Wege nach Basel noch in München sich beim
Führer unmittelbar in einer halbstündigen Aussprache
den Auftrag ausdrücklich wiederholen lassen.

Auf meinen Einwand, Präsident Schacht
habe von der ganzen Absicht vor Antritt seiner Reise
den Reichsaußenminister nicht unterrichtet, erwiderte
Schacht, hierzu hätte er nach der Anlage der Reise
keine Zeit gehabt, auchwenn er das Auswärtige Amt für
zuständig gehalten hätte.

(gez.) Weizsäcker

18

OFFICE OF CHIEF OF COUNSEL
FOR WAR CRIMES
APO 696-A   U.S.ARMY

STAFF EVIDENCE ANALYSIS, Ministries Division.

By: Mark Schafer
Date: 23 April 1947

Document Number: NG-1518

Title and/or general nature: Note by WEIZSAECKER regardings a
                                     demand by SCHACHT for authorization
                                     to continue his Rublee-discussions[1]

Form of Document: Typed original

Stamps and other endorsements: Signature of WEIZSAECKER.
                                     Initials of WOERMANN.

Date: 4 January 1939

Source: "3216 26 Judenfrage U.St.S.
                                     24 Nr. 2";
                                     now at: FO-SD, Building 32,
                                     MDB, Berlin.
                                     (OCC BBT 1087)

PERSONS OR ORGANIZATIONS IMPLICATED:
                                     WEIZSAECKER
                                     WOERMANN
                                     ALBRECHT
                                     SCHACHT

Doc. 6

19

TO BE FILED UNDER THESE REFERENCE HEADINGS:
                                     NG - Foreign Office
                                     NG - Political and Racial
                                          Persecution
                                     NG - Ministry of Economics

SUMMARY:
      WEIZSAECKER reports that SCHACHT has contacted him by
telephone and questioned him with regard to an earlier call,
wherein WEIZSAECKER apparently had challenged the authority of
SCHACHT to conduct the London discussions regarding the
emigration of Jews from Germany. SCHACHT had insisted that
HITLER was satisfied with the progress of the discussions,
and he intended now to see RIBBENTROP on the matter.

      WEIZSAECKER concludes the note with the following
phrase: "I have intentionally refrained from questioning
SCHACHT with regard to the contents of his London talks and
the material basis on which he intends to continue these
talks with RUBLEE".

[1]
 Analyst's note: Discussions conducted in London between
SCHACHT and RUBLEE regarding the emigration of Jews from
Germany.)

E N D

Berlin, den 4. Januar 1939.

Präsident S c h a c h t kam heute telefonisch
auf meinen kürzlichen Anruf zurück, worin ich ihm die Frage nach seiner Autorisation zu den Rublee-Besprechungen gestellt hatte. Herr Schacht sagt, er habe dem Führer vor-
gestern Vortrag gehalten. Der Führer sei mit seinen -
Schacht's - Besprechungen in London einverstanden gewesen und habe ihn mit der Fortsetzung beauftragt. Schacht
will nunmehr Rublee hierher bestellen.

Um seiner mir kürzlich gegebenen Zusage zu ent-
sprechen möchte der Präsident heute oder morgen oder am
Sonnabend dem Herrn Reichsminister über seine Londoner
Unterhaltungen mündlich Bericht erstatten.

Nachdem ich dem Präsidenten die Dispositionen
des Herrn Reichsministers mitgeteilt hatte, schlug Schacht
Sonnabend für seinen Besuch bei dem Herrn Reichsminister
vor. Am Sonnabend Nachmittag scheint er zu einer Monats-
sitzung nach Basel zu verreisen.

Ich habe es absichtlich unterlassen, Schacht
nach dem Inhalt seiner Gespräche in London und nach der
sachlichen Grundlage zu fragen, auf welcher er nun mit
Rublee weiter verhandeln will.

gez: Weizsäcker

Herrn Reichsminister
(Büro: bitte nach München
nachtelefonieren)
Herrn Unterstaatssekretär
Herrn Dg. Pol.
Herrn Dir. W.
Herrn Dir. Recht

321658

II 112

Do/Be   23.1.39.

T a g e s m e l d u n g

Betr.: Evian-Konferenz.

Doc. 7

        Aus jüdischer Quelle wird bekannt, daß am
23.Januar in Paris das Evian-Komitee und drei Tage
darauf in London die Vollversammlung der Evian-Mächte
zusammentreten. Beiden Gremien werden die Berichte
der befragten Staaten vorliegen, aus denen hervorgeht,
ob und welchen Anfall an Juden sie aufzunehmen bereit
sind.

21

                                        II 112
                                        i.V. [Unterschrift]

[handschriftlicher Vermerk] *Vermerk*
Maj. Hirth wurde tel. verst.

II 112

25.1.1939

Hg/Be

T a g e s m e l d u n g

Die arabische Delegation für die Round Table Konferenz in
London ist gestern abgereist. Neben den Vertretern der ver-
schiedenen arabischen Länder sind auch zwei von den Engländern
bestimmte Vertreter für die Nashashibi Partei abgereist.
(Der Mufti hatte sich für die Entsendung einer solchen
Oppositionsgruppe bereit erklärt) Wie bekannt wird, hat sich
Nashashibi, der in Kairo verblieben ist, mit dieser Delegation
nicht einverstanden erklärt, zumal der eine Teilnehmer schon
seit längerer Zeit nicht mehr Mitglied seiner Partei ist.

Ägypten ist durch Ali Maher, den Präsidenten des Kronrates,
einen Prinzen des königlichen Hauses und den Gesandten in
London vertreten.

Die Beförderung nach London erfolgt auf einem englischen
Dampfer. Soweit bekannt, werden die Transportkosten von
den Engländern getragen.

II 112

22

G $\dfrac{\text{II 112}}{69}$

14.2.1939

Hg./Hrt.

T a g e s m e l d u n g :

23

Von einem zuverlässigen V-Mann wird bekannt, dass der englische Gesandte in Prag nach angeblicher Befragung des Intelligence Service dem Innenministerium gegenüber zu verstehen gegeben hat, dass die gegen eine illegale Einwanderung von Juden in Palästina keine Einwände erheben./Abgabe einer schriftlichen Erklärung wurde jedoch abgelehnt.

In diesem Zusammenhang wird weiterhin bekannt, dass sich das englische Reisebüro Cook in Prag bereiterklärt hat, illegale Transporte nach Palästina unter seinem Namen durch den hier bekannten Griechen Konstantin Nikolopoulos, der mit dem Melder in Verbindung steht, durchführen zu lassen.

Daraus kann geschlossen werden, dass England bemüht ist eine Palästina-Lösung im Sinne des Judentums zu finden.

II 112

SS-H'Stuf.

G $\frac{\text{II } 112}{69}$

16.Februar 1939

Prö.

T a g e s m e l d u n g .
===

Nach einer Meldung des "Jüdischen Nachrichtenblattes" ist
Juden der Eintritt in die "Front der Nationalen Wieder-
geburt" in Rumänien verboten.

Jüdisches Nachrichtenblatt, v. 17.2.39

"Nach einer Meldung aus Sofia hat die bulgarische Polizei
auf Anordnung des Innenministeriums über 6 000 Juden fremder Staatsangehörigkeit mit einer Frist von vierzehn
Tagen aus Bulgarien ausgewiesen. Das Kriegsministerium
hat Juden als Lieferanten für das Heer ohne Ausnahme aus-
geschlossen."

Wie der "Verband polnischer Juden e.V." Berlin bekannt
gibt, müssen alle Anträge auf Einreisegenehmigung der
nach Polen abgeschobenen Juden auf Grund des deutsch-pol-
nischen Abkommens bis zum 21.II.d.J. gestellt sein. Der
letzte Einreisetermin nach Deutschland ist der 31.Juli 1939.

II 112

G <u>II 112</u>
69   21. Februar 1939

Prö.

            T a g e s m e l d u n g .
            ×============================

        Am 13. Februar tagte das Evian-Komitee in London. Mr.Myron
C. T a y l o r gab bekannt, dass die Philippinen jährlich tausend
Einwanderer aufnehmen.Er berichtete über die Entsendung dreier
Kommissionen, einer nach Britisch Guayana, einer nach San Domingo,
und einer nach den Philippinen, die die Einwanderungsmöglich -
keiten überprüfen sollen. Lord Winterton erklärte , Großbritannien
sei kein Einwanderungsland. Der bisherige Vorsitzende des Evian-
Komitees, Rublee, ist zurückgetreten. An seiner Stelle übernimmt
Sir Herbert Emerson den Vorsitz.

        Das Evianer Komitee billigte <u>einen Plan zur Schaffung einer</u>
<u>privaten internationalen Körperschaft, der die Auswanderung der</u>
<u>Juden aus Deutschland und ihre Ansiedlung in anderen Ländern</u>
<u>finanzieren soll.</u>Das Komitee beschloss, in einer Erklärung fest-
zulegen, dass der Ausschuss sein äußerstes tun werde, um inner -
halb von 5 Jahren für alle Auswanderer aus Deutschland eine Heim-
stätte zu finden. Die internationale Körperschaft wird ein rein
privates Unternehmen sein, das sich in der Hauptsache aus jüdisch
aber auch anderen Finanzleuten zusammensetzt. Man erwartet, dass
diese Korporation die Aufnahme einer großen Anleihe veranlassen
wird. Als Sicherheit für diese Anleihen werden vielleicht die
Naturschätze in den unentwickelten Kolonialgebieten, in denen die
Einwanderer angesiedelt werden, benutztwerden.

        Der Abgeordnete Jozwiak legte dem Sejm zwei Gesetzesanträg
vor, Der erste soll den Juden, die nach dem 11.November 1918 in
die Staatsbürgerliste eingetragen wurden, die Abänderung ihres
Familiennamens verbieten. Der zweite sieht die Beschaffung von
Räumlichkeiten auch im Wege der Requirierung für die polnische
Bevölkerung vor.

                            II 112
                            i.A.

G II 112   7.3.39
   69

                T a g e s m e l d u n g .
         ===================================

        Nach Meldung eines hiesigen V.-Mannes ist angeblich im
26   Schwarzen Meer der griechische Dampfer "Cepo", der 780 illegale
     jüdische Auswanderer an Bord hatte, untergegangen. Nach Meldung
     der Zentralstelle für jüd.Auswanderung,Wien war kein ~~österreichisch~~
             aus Österreich   ~~er~~
     Jude~~n~~an Bord.

                                    II 112

T a g e s m e l d u n g .
■■■■■■■■■■■■■■■■■■■■■■■■■■■■

Lord Winterton, der Vorsitzende des Evian-Komitees, erklärte
anlässlich einer Rede in Devonport,die Vereinigten Staaten
hätten durch die Aufnahme jüdischer Einwanderer aus
Deutschland, von Juli 1938 bis Juli 1939 30.000 bis 40.000,
wesentlich zur Lösung des jüdischen Wanderungsproblems
beigetragen.Australien würde 5.000 Menschen im gleichen
Zeitraum das Niederlassungsrecht gewähren.

Das Britische Kolonial-Ministerium gibt bekannt, dass sich
eine Experten-Kommission nach Nord-Rhodesien begeben habe.
Es soll festgestellt werden, in welchen Distrikten Aus -
wanderer aus europäischen Ländern angesiedelt werden
können und was für ein geldlicher Aufwand erforderlich
wäre. Der Kommission wird der Jude A.Khasanof von der
Palästine Jewish Colonization Association (Pica) angehören.

                    II 112-Pr.

G $\frac{II\ 1120}{69}$ 27.4.39

T a g e s m e l d u n g .
=============================

Die Jewish Agency bestreitet in einem Schreiben an den
High Commissioner die rechtliche Gültigkeit des neuen
Einwanderungserlasses für Palästina.Der Erlass sei mit
den internationalen Verpflichtungen der Mandatarmacht
nicht in Einklang zu bringen.

In Frankreich wurde zur Zentralisierung der Unterbringung
jüdischer Kinder in Frankreich das "Comité israélite pour
les enfants" unter dem Präsidium der Baronin Eduard von
Rothschild geschaffen. Das Comité arbeitet mit dem American
Joint Distribution Comittee zusammen.

                                   II 112
                                i.V.

MEETING OF OFFICERS

of the

INTER-GOVERNMENTAL COMMITTEE ON POLITICAL REFUGEES

Department of State,
Washington, D. C.
October 17, 1939 - 3 p.m.

- - - - - -

PRESENT:

Hon. Cordell Hull, Secretary of State.

The Rt. Hon. The Earl Winterton, Paymaster General
in the United Kingdom Government, Chairman;
accompanied by Messrs. Bramwell and Alington,
Advisers.

His Excellency Senor Don Felipe A. Espil, Ambassador
of the Argentine Republic.

His Excellency Mr. Carlos Martins, Ambassador of
Brazil.

His Excellency Count de Saint-Quentin, Ambassador
of the French Republic, accompanied by
M. Jacques Dumaine, Adviser.

The Hon. Dr. A. Loudon, Minister of the Netherlands,
accompanied by Mr. A.F.H. Van Troostenburg de
Bruyn, Adviser.

Doc. 8

29

Hon. Myron C. Taylor, Vice-Chairman, Inter-
Governmental Committee, representing the
United States of America, accompanied by
Mr. Robert Pell, Adviser.

Hon. James G. McDonald, Chairman, President's
Advisory Committee on Political Refugees,
accompanied by Mr. George L. Warren, Executive Secretary, President's Advisory
Committee on Political Refugees.

Mr. Stephen Morris, Acting Secretary, Inter-
Governmental Committee on Political
Refugees.

30

Hon. Cordell Hull:

Gentlemen: On behalf of this Government I am glad to extend a most hearty welcome to each of you who comprise this organization.

We are particularly appreciative of those who have come some distance under more or less inconvenience to be present on this occasion. It manifests a far-reaching interest which should afford encouragement to all of us who may need encouragement in this connection.

You are engaged in a most righteous undertaking, an undertaking that involves not only the highest and the finest exhibition of humanitarianism and of civilized human effort, but you typify law and order at a time when a vast portion of the world is in a sea of international anarchy, and stand for constructive thought and action when so many destructive forces are abroad.

31

You assemble in an undertaking that is worthy in the highest sense, and you assemble at a most critical period in the history of our civilized life.

The occasion and the problem recall some of the noble thoughts of the most trying periods in the history of the human race.

It has been said that "man's inhumanity to man makes countless thousands mourn".

Again, "These are days that try men's souls".

I might repeat many of those soul-stirring statements to which great patriots, great humanitarians, have given spontaneous utterance in the ages that are past.

We do know that at this period there are an increasing number of people who are draining the cup of bitterness and of disappointment to its very dregs. We do know that they are on a level below that of the common animal, which is able to find something on which to subsist, to find some place where it can rest and relax and sleep. We know that these unfortunate people who have been made outcasts are without a country, without a home, without a family, without any means of subsistence. The more we ponder on this ordinarily unthinkable situation and condition of an increasing number of unfortunate human souls, the more we are stirred to the utmost to find ways to solve this problem. We have this condition, we have this staggering problem that is presented, which is a challenge to law and order and decency, as well as a challenge to every humanitarian instinct.

That is why I feel all the greater pride and the greater thanks go out to each of the Governments participating in the Committee which, moved at an early stage, have consecrated time and effort to a suitable approach and an effective solution of the terrific problem.

I know that the thanks of the civilized millions in every part of the world will increase, as understanding and appreciation of your work is more fully impressed upon them. I know that you will leave nothing undone that it may be possible to do in keeping alive a movement intended to grapple with this ever-increasing problem. I think it would be most unfortunate if future historians should be called upon to say that civilized man confessed his inability to cope with this harrowing problem and let the undertaking die at its most critical period.

I sat down here merely for the purpose of saying welcome and wishing you God-speed. I am sorry that I am not able to sit at your feet here and learn more about this problem, in order that I might consecrate myself more effectively in the future to its solution.

I take great pleasure in turning the meeting over to the Chairman, Lord Winterton.

Lord Winterton: I hope that you will allow me on my own behalf and on behalf of all my colleagues to thank you most sincerely for the speech which you have just delivered.

I should like to say, speaking on behalf of my Government, and I imagine that my colleagues would like to join with me on behalf of their Governments, that we are deeply grateful to the President of the United States and to your Government for giving us this opportunity of discussing these difficult problems.

It only remains for me to add that all of us, I think, are most anxious to see some solution of this great problem

33

and to say that since this Committee was first formed in
July 1938 that the thirty-two countries represented upon
it, and especially those countries which supply the officers of the organization, the Vice Chairmen and the organization have worked in the greatest amity and harmony.
Naturally we should have liked to have achieved more. I
think we can say, however, that, thanks very largely to our
two directors, Mr. George Rublee and Sir Herbert Emerson,
we can claim that in that comparatively short period we
have done something to alleviate human suffering and to
bring order out of chaos.

(Applause)

34

(At this point Lord Winterton took the Chair and
Secretary Hull left the meeting).

Lord Winterton: I will ask Mr. Myron Taylor if he will
now address the conference.

Mr. Myron Taylor: Mr. Chairman and gentlemen:

I would like to say first of all what a very great
pleasure it is to me to have you, Lord Winterton, and you,
Sir Herbert Emerson, in Washington for a meeting of the
Intergovernmental Committee. I realize the difficulties
which might have persuaded less courageous souls to remain
at home at the present time, but you have overlooked all
danger and difficulty that might come to you, and we are
delighted to have you with us.

You and your government have been so hospitable to us
of the committee during the last year, that it is a satisfaction to reciprocate your hospitality in some small
measure.

The President at the opening of our conference today
emphasized that the committee has a duty to look into the
future, determine what must be done to continue the work in
behalf of refugees, despite the outbreak of the war.

For our guidance he has set forth several high points.

First, the President said that the work of the
committee should not be abandoned, it must be re-directed.

Second, he suggested that urgent attention should be
given to the short range program for dealing with persons
who are now in countries of refuge. He said that this
program involves the resettlement of somewhat more than
100,000 persons who were craving an opportunity to resume
a useful life.

Third, he said that a long range program should be envisaged for dealing with the broader problem of resettling
great numbers of people who may be victims of the war.

Fourth, the President emphasized the importance of going ahead in an active manner with the engineering and
colonizing aspects of settlement projects.

Fifth, the President expressed the hope that the
governments members of the Intergovernmental Committee
would be consulted with regard to the possibility of

extending the activity of the committee.

I am confident there will be no difference of opinion with regard to continuing the work of the Intergovernmental Committee. The committee has proved its value in trying times. I am sure that it will continue to be of service in a time of international catastrophe. I am certain that this point will not require discussion.

In regard to the second point, that is the necessity of the short range program for dealing with persons in countries of temporary refuge, I am sure that we shall welcome the expert opinions of Sir Herbert Emerson and of Monsieur van Zeeland. All reports which we have received indicate that the situation of refugees in these countries is acute, and that it is urgently necessary to take steps to alleviate this situation.

I believe that this can be done partly by a continuation of the processes of infiltration. It must be supplemented, however, by a beginning of settlement in the various places which have been explored and upon which work can now begin.

What the committee can do to solve the broader general problem of refugees will depend in large part upon whether the governments members of the committee are willing to extend the activity of the committee. We shall have to consider this point carefully and determine how we can proceed with the best promise of positive results.

It is clear that we, the officers, cannot bind the committee. All that we can do is to report to the participating governments that President Roosevelt has expressed the hope that the committee's mandate could be extended, and invite expressions of their respective views.

I would like to suggest that the chairman instruct the secretary to circularize the participating governments immediately to this effect, and to correlate the replies for the information of the officers and the full committee.

In conclusion may I urge that there be no let up in the work which we have undertaken and in the exemplary work of the coordinating foundation and the individual corporations for dealing with the respective settlement projects.

I fully realize that the war has greatly complicated our task, and that, for example, the transit countries which heretofore have played such an important part in accepting refugees temprarily, are no longer in position to do so, and that private communities are no longer able to contribute their share of relief funds that are required. This will necessitate, among other things, moving emigrants hereafter directly to the countries of settlement. I cite only this one example.

There are other factors which complicate the situation, but we must not evidence discouragement, we must bend our backs to the task of greater vigor and prove that we have the foresight and ingenuity required to solve the problem

37

which is a blot on our Western civilization.

Lord Winterton: His Excellency, the Ambassador from Argentine, Senor Don Felipe A. Espil.

His Excellency Senor Espil (Argentine Republic): I have no special comment to make although I wish to pay tribute to the great humanitarian undertaking sponsored by President Roosevelt.

Lord Winterton: Does the Brazilian Ambassador wish to say a few words? His Excellency Carlos Martins, Ambassador from Brazil.

His Excellency Senor Carlos Martins (Brazil): I have no particular instructions from my government about this.

I wish to express the full appreciation of my government, however.

Lord Winterton: The French Ambassador, Count de Saint-Quentin.

His Excellency Count de Saint-Quentin (France): For myself I must apologize for not being very familiar with those problems, but I, of course, want to express the deep interest which our government takes in that problem and the work of this committee.

My first duty would be, of course, to say how deeply the French representatives on this Committee regrets not being here. Mr. Myron Taylor told us at the luncheon of the telegram which he had received from Monsieur Henry Berenger. Being, as you know, the Chairman of the Committee on Foreign Affairs of the French Senate, my eminent compatriot is detained at home and could not emulate Lord Winterton's example, as he should like to have done.

As you know, France has always been, in the course of history, familiar with the refugee problem. On account of our geographical situation, and also perhaps from our national character, or maybe that our geographical situation has influenced our national character, it has been quite a tradition for France to accept on her territory and to welcome a great number of foreigners.

We have now, out of a population of nearly 40,000,000 inhabitants, about 3,000,000 foreigners. Those foreigners are at home, they feel comfortable on our soil, and they certainly contribute to the prosperity of the country.

In that number are included several hundred thousand political refugees, people who have been advised to leave their own country because they weren't acceptable any more to the prevailing race or creed or political school.

We have consistently accorded this hospitality in the course of our history, and we have found it a contribution to our people, to the intellectual and moral formation of the French nation, that means to our civilization, and that has been very great.

I think now we may have about 500,000 political refugees, some of whom came gradually after the war, about 75,000 White Russians, about 65,000 Armenians, a good many Austrians and Germans, when we had the second wave, if I may say so, of

39

Germans and Austrians, especially people of Jewish creed, but also a good many Catholics or Protestants who disagreed with the political doctrines of the German Government.

Those people were there when we had the unprecedented influx of 400,000 Spanish refugees.

Of course, this Committee has been especially mandated to deal with the question of the German and Austrian people. So we are quite sympathetic to the appeal that the President and the American Government sent to the nations to study the problem of resettling those refugees of Central Europe. Among those who have been admitted in France, a good many are waiting departure for other countries, having applied for a visa to enter the United States or some other country.

A special problem has arisen in regard to them since the outbreak of the present war. Many of them are German and Austrian citizens. That means that independently of their own feelings and their creeds, they are subjects of an enemy power and have had to be interned in special camps. The only way to deal with such cases was to have a general roundup at first, but we have already begun to open the doors to some people we knew very well and who offered every guarantee. I am informed by my Government that it is its intention to open the doors still wider and to help those people to return little by little to normal life.....That process may be hastened thanks to the valuable cooperation of such an organization as O.R.T. which, as you know, has

40

devoted its activity for many years to the professional training of refugees.....I think that France will thus be able to assist settlement countries, because it will furnish them with people who won't interfere with the local economy, as they would be not only tradesmen and bankers or doctors, a surplus of which seems to exist in many countries, but also agricultural workers or skilled workers.

Under the present conditions, as Mr. Myron Taylor reminded us, we should find it very difficult for the Government to give any financial contribution to the plan finally agreed on by the committee, but of course we shall do our best in full sympathy and agreement with the other members of the Committee, and, I may add, in deep gratitude to the American Government and the American people who have been so generous towards the refugees of all countries and whose example is, I feel, so comforting to refugees in all parts of the world. We can't indeed forget that among the original settlers of this great country there were a good many refugees that came from our European countries.

That is all as to the immediate problem that Mr. Myron Taylor spoke of.

As for the larger problem, I have no special instructions. I shall communicate with my Government, but I must say that we greatly appreciate that the interest of the American Government goes above the present time to the future. War absorbs all the activities of the countries unfortunately

41

engaged in it. However, we must try to see above it, and go on in the pursuit of our ideals.

Lord Winterton: I am going to ask the Minister of the Kingdom of the Netherlands if he will address us, the Honorable Doctor A. Loudon.

The Honorable Dr. A. Loudon (Netherlands): In the first place, I would like to refer to the general remarks made by Mr. Beucker-Andreae with regard to this problem, and which are to be found in the minutes of the Evian Conference. The situation, so far as the Netherlands are concerned, has not changed since that time.

I think, therefore, I need not take your time by giving a second general picture of this problem.

Nor do I think it is necessary because I entirely agree, and I know that the Netherlands Government entirely agrees, with the picture that has just been given by the French Ambassador, concerning the moral side of the question.

I listened to the President's speech during the luncheon at the White House with a great deal of interest, and it seems to me that the President has raised quite a few new questions. With regard to these new questions, to which Mr. Myron Taylor has alluded, I have no instructions from my Government. My instructions apply only to the agenda which is before us, and I can therefore give my Government's views only with regard to the items on the agenda.

42

In the meantime, I think that the address of the
President of the United States has been so inspiring that
I am of the opinion that it deserves our closest attention.
I therefore venture to suggest that we divide our work
in two, and dedicate ourselves first to the agenda and
then to the new points which both the President of the
United States and Mr. Myron Taylor brought forth.

These new points could be discussed in some way, and
might perhaps be formed in the shape of a draft resolution or a wish, to be submitted at once to our respective
governments, either directly by us or through the inter-
mediary of the full committee.

I must leave that entirely to you, Mr. Chairman,
but I think that we should not lose time as the President
has stressed that it is very necessary to do something,
and that we should go to work at once. In that way
perhaps we can defer to the wishes of the President and
give proof of our interest in what he has said.

Lord Winterton: Gentlemen, as the Chairman of the
Intergovernmental Committee, I have heard with great
interest what my colleagues around the table have said.

Perhaps I might deal with the point that Dr. Loudon
has just raised, and say that it seems to me that probably
the procedure that he suggests will be the best procedure.
The importance of the question which was raised by the
President in his address at lunch cannot be overestimated,

and I have not received any definite instructions from my Government upon the point. I think that probably we all feel that we should confer with our Governments and receive our instructions before we can make a very definite statement on the matter, and I have rather gathered, Mr. Taylor, that that would be also the view of the United States Government.

Mr. Taylor: In the statement I made I suggested that reference be had to the Governments, and as you were speaking I was questioning myself whether in the first instance the officers, the chairman and the vice chairmen, and the director, should consult with their governments on these points before presenting the points to the full committee.

I wonder how you would feel about that, Mr. Chairman?

Lord Winterton: I think that would probably be the most convenient course and I don't want to trouble my colleagues with a long statement, but I think that I should be wanting in courtesy to the United States Government if I did not say a word in commendation of what has recently been done.

When more than a year ago, the British and other Governments responded to the generous initiative of the United States Government in calling a conference for the purpose of dealing with the problem of refugees from Germany, they little thought that, heart-breaking though that problem was, it was to be made vastly more distressing, wider and more complicated by a war which none of the countries represented at Evian desired, and which some of them, now involved in it, desperately attempted to ward off. In spite of the efforts of my Government, on which it is unnecessary for me to dwell, to promote a peaceful settlement of the disputed issues in European politics, war broke out and is raging with an intensity which needs no emphasis from me. I will only say that the same forces which gave rise to the original problem which the Evian Committee was called into being to deal with have set in motion powers of destruction to meet which all the peoples of Europe, whether directly involved in the war or not, will need all the courage and fortitude they possess to withstand, if the Christian civilization on which so much of the world's life depends is not to be overwhelmed.

In such a welter of hatred and destruction, amid such immeasurable and undeserved human suffering, the continued sympathy of your great country towards the refugees in this problem is a factor whose significance it would be impossible to exaggerate.

Such a gesture, inspired by charity and a sense of human brotherhood transcending all political considerations will not, however, have come as unexpected to the members of the Committee. I may be allowed briefly to recall that in the vast refugee problems created in the war that began in 1914, it was the United States who took the most prominent part in initiating, organizing and carrying on relief among

45

refugees of various nationalities on a scale to which we
have not yet come, but which we should perhaps be unwise to
dismiss as impossible as the struggle develops. If I say
that the American Red Cross in March 1923 is recorded to
have been feeding half a million refugees a day - one
example among many which might be quoted from 1914 on-
wards - this will indicate something of the boundless generosity and gift for organization applied by the American
people to the victims of war, revolution and persecution.

The human appeal to which the United States responded
so nobly has been heard also by the British and other nations.
Speaking for my own people I can say that from the time when
the refugee problem became a matter of serious international
concern, there was a wave of generous sentiment, expressed
not only in hospitality and financial assistance, but in
whole-hearted support from all political parties to His
Majesty's Government in the various measures which they proposed in an effort to solve the problem or at least alleviate
some of its most distressing consequences. I need only
mention the large sums voted for the assistance of refugees
from Czechoslovakia, and the offer which, on behalf of
my Government I was authorized to make to the Inter-Governmental Committee last July, that they were prepared to consider contributions from public funds to the cost of refugee
settlement. That offer was made, not only in time of peace,
but at a time when it appeared as if the labors of the Inter-

Governmental Committee were going to bear fruit in a practical scheme for the orderly emigration from Germany. With
the coming of the immeasurable disaster of war the situation
is fundamentally altered. Not all the original function of
the Committee is destroyed; it still has tasks, perhaps
bigger tasks, before it. But the financial resources at
least of those member-Governments which have to bear the
burden of a mighty struggle are now fully pledged to the
prosecution of the war, in which they are engaging their
blood and their treasure. Projects which His Majesty's
Government in the United Kingdom were anxious to promote
are now rendered extremely difficult, if not impossible of
execution. Yet, in spite of all, thanks to the initiative
taken by the American Government, the basis of international
cooperation remains; the will to work together in an effort
to solve the refugee problem is still alive, and we can all
devote our thoughts to considering what has so far been
achieved, what has been planned and what it may, under new
conditions, be possible still to plan for the effective
furtherance of the great cause in whose service you have
called us together. On behalf of my Government I want to
say that we will, in a spirit of complete frankness, but
with the utmost sympathy and desire to collaborate, examine
any suggestions which may be made during this conference,
with the object of alleviating the distress, and more,
promoting a lasting settlement of the tremendous difficulties

47

caused by the refugee problem in Europe.

Gentlemen, I think you will agree that the next step that we should take would be to ask our director, Sir Herbert Emerson, to report to us what has taken place since the last meeting of the full Intergovernmental Committee.

Sir Herbert, will you address the conference?

Sir Herbert Emerson: Just a general statement of the situation, or on the first item in the agenda?

Lord Winterton: Mr. Pell, what were your ideas in drawing that up?

Mr. Pell: We understood that Sir Herbert had a statement which he wanted to make.

Sir Herbert Emerson: Well, perhaps I may explain --

Lord Winterton: (interposing) Perhaps Sir Herbert's statement would come best on the first item of the agenda. Is that the wish of the conference? And then I understand it has been suggested that Mr. McDonald should make a statement after Sir Herbert has spoken. I think that would all come in item 1 of the agenda. I take it, gentlemen, that we agree on that. Sir Herbert, will you then open the discussion on the first item of the agenda today, which is the "Report on the present position of the refugee problem and a review of the work of the Intergovernmental Committee".

Sir Herbert Emerson: I may say that I have written a memorandum on each of the first five items on the agenda.

Owing to the war it was not possible to communicate the
memoranda direct to the individual officers, but I had
hoped that a copy might be in their hands before this
meeting. With that object in view, I had sent to the
American Embassy in London copies of the memoranda with the
request that the State Department would be good enough to
deliver them to the representatives. The ship by which the
memoranda came, left, I believe, four days before we left,
but unfortunately for the memoranda, and happily for us,
we have arrived before the memoranda.

I must therefore apologize that copies of them are not
in the hands of the representatives, and unfortunately
I have myself with me today only one copy. I shall refer
briefly to this memorandum which I shall place later at the
disposal of the officers. (Sir Herbert Emerson then gave
the substance of the memorandum, the full text of which is
given below):

MEMORANDUM
by the Director

1.   In view of the war, it is unnecessary to give more
than a very brief statement of the relations between the
Intergovernmental Committee and the German authorities
immediately before the outbreak of hostilities. The conversations carried on in January and February of this year resulted in an expression of the intention of the German
Government to carry out a program of orderly emigration,

49

provided that substantial progress was made in the settlement of involuntary migrants in other countries. The program provided for the release of Jews from concentration camps, for the restraining of persons for emigration, for the employment of persons awaiting emigration, for the finance, subject to certain conditions, of emigration from Jewish funds in Germany, for the removal from Germany by involuntary migrants of personal property and equipment for resettlement, and for exemption from emigration taxes. The Intergovernmental Committee, at its February meeting, took cognizance of this program, and decided that it would, acting independently, continue to exert its best efforts to develop opportunities for settlement. During the spring and summer months of this year several occasions were taken to impress on Herr Wohlthat the magnitude of the migration then taking place from Germany and the progress that was being made in solving the problem of involuntary emigration from Germany. Certain provisions of the German program were put into effect. The number detained in concentration camps was greatly reduced. Some measures were taken to provide retraining for emigration, restrictions on the employment of Jews were relaxed in some respects, and a central organization for the relief and education of Jews inside Germany was established. No effective steps, however, were taken to establish the Internal Trust inside Germany, which was to be the authority through which the emigration was to

50

be financially assisted. In my last discussion, however, with Herr Wohlthat on July 19th last, definite hope was expressed that there would be little further delay in its establishment, and a later message suggested that it would be set up within a month. Before the month had expired the crisis which developed into the present war had darkened the entire outlook and made further progress impracticable.

2.   Before the outbreak of war I drafted a memorandum describing the position of the refugee problem as it was at the end of August. This memorandum is now out of date, since the nature of the problem has changed to a large extent, but I repeat such facts and figures contained in the original memorandum as may be relevant or of interest.

51

(a) Making use of material from various sources I estimated that at the end of August, 1939, the number of confessional Jews in Germany was 250,000 and in Austria 63,000, making a total of 313,000. Had the war not occurred it would have been necessary to emigrate 167,000 of these from Germany and 42,000 from Austria.

(b) The total number of non-Aryan Christians in Greater Germany was 190,000 at a rough estimate, of whom 127,000 would have had to be evacuated.

(c) The Council for German Jewry made an estimate of the total emigration of confessional Jews from Greater Germany between April 1933 and July 1, 1939. The figures were as follows:

From Germany	215,000
From Austria	97,000
From Czecho-Slovakia	17,000
Total	329,000

Those evacuated from Czecho-Slovakia consisted almost entirely of Jewish refugees from Germany, Austria or the Sudetenland. On the assumption that the emigration of non-Aryan Christians has been roughly one-fifth of that of full Jews, and allowing for emigration since the Council for German Jewry made its estimate, it may be assumed that, since 1933, 400,000 refugees have emigrated from Greater Germany.

(d) The Council for German Jewry estimated that, of the number of full Jews who had emigrated from Germany up to July 1, 1939, 150,000 were in European countries, that of these 50,000 could be considered as settled, and that not less than 100,000 were awaiting re-emigration. To these might be added 20,000 non-Aryan Christians and about the same number of Czechs and political refugees from the Sudetenland. The Council for German Jewry further estimated that, of the Jewish refugees who have found refuge in countries outside Europe, 16,000 would have to be re-emigrated. Had there been no war, the problem of emigration within the scope of the mandate of the Intergovernmental Committee would have been as follows:

(1) To be emigrated from Germany - confessional Jews - 167,000.

(2)　To be emigrated from Austria – confessional
Jews – 42,000.

(3)　To be emigrated from Greater Germany non-Aryan
Christians – 127,000.

(4)　To be re-emigrated from European countries of
temporary refuge – 140,000.

(5)　To be re-emigrated from non-European countries
of temporary refuge – 16,000.

3.　Mention may be made of certain features of the
position as it existed at the end of August.

(a)　Practically all the well-to-do refugees with resources outside Germany had already left; so had most of
those who had relatives or friends outside Germany able to
support them or to give the necessary guarantee. Again,
where emigration has been governed by the selection of suitable persons, as in the case of some countries of settlement,
the process has removed many of those most suitable for
emigration. It is therefore reasonable to suppose that those
still in Germany are on the whole poorer in material resources and weaker in personal qualifications than those
who have left. Even before the war neighbouring countries
had closed their frontiers so far as this could be done.
Shanghai was no longer a place of refuge, and insofar as
illegal entry into Palestine was successful, it was set
off by a reduction in the number of legal entrants. These
were all factors which would have operated against the

53

maintenance of the past rate of emigration. On the other hand, there was a snowball element in the movement, which was producing intangible but very considerable results. As the refugees became settled in new countries and able to provide for others, one of their first acts was to secure the emigration of their relatives, and this process had a cumulative effect which continuously tended to accelerate emigration.

(b)   While the number of persons to be evacuated from Germany was continuously decreasing, the number of those to be re-emigrated from countries of temporary refuge was continuously increasing. My estimate of the number of these at the end of August, 1939 was 156,000, of whom 140,000 were in European countries. This latter number, it may be observed, was not the total in those countries, which was nearer 200,000. Of the total, at least 60,000 were dependent for maintenance on charitable organizations, and this was also the case with the great majority of the 16,000 who would have to be re-emigrated from non-European countries of temporary refuge. On the other hand, had there been no war, a considerable number of those in European countries would have been able to finance their own emigration had openings been available, and the Council for German Jewry put the number of these as high as 50,000. Before the war the problem of refugees in countries of temporary refuge was a serious one. It was an embarrassment to the Government concerned, it was viewed with suspicion by organized labor, and, although much of this suspicion was founded on false economics, it none the less increased the danger of anti-semitism. Further, it placed a tremendous strain on the resources of the private organizations, which were finding themselves unable to furnish the funds for maintenance and at the same time to finance emigration. Already both in Holland and Belgium the State had been obliged to come to the assistance of the organizations in maintaining the refugees.

(c) It was recognized that the problem of Jews in Greater Germany was a part only of the general question of Jews in Central Europe. There was a widespread movement, based on economic, political or racial grounds, and affect-ing Poland, Roumania, Hungary and Bulgaria, to reduce by emigration the Jewish population. The intensity of the pressure in each of these countries varied with political conditions, but where economic factors were at work as in Poland, the problem was largely independent of political causes. The pressure was greatest where German influence was high, and since the events of March 1939 there had been serious and steady deterioration in the position of Jews in Bohemia, Moravia and Slovakia. The position in the Pro-tectorate and Slovakia was particularly relevant, since it was closely connected with German policy and the German program. Briefly, the position was as follows: In the Protectorate there were 100,000 confessional Jews, of whom approximately 15,000 came directly within the mandate of the Intergovernmental Committee as being refugees from Germany, Austria and the Sudetenland. In addition there were between 10,000 and 15,000 non-Aryan Christians. In Slovakia there were roughly 90,000 Jews of whom 5,000 were refugees from other countries. Under German influence and pressure the persecution of Jews had already reached ser- ious proportions. In the Protectorate, the Jewish leaders had been ordered by the German authorities to arrange for the emigration of Jews at the rate of 1000 per week. No funds were available from private organizations, except a little from the Jewish Agency, and the balance of the British Government Fund was quite inadequate to finance emigration except on a small scale. If, therefore, there had been no war, and persecution had made it necessary to take up the question of Jewish emigration from the Protectorate and Slovakia, it would have been necessary proportionately to curtail the German program for Greater Germany.

4. Some attempt may now be made to appraise the drastic changes in the problem caused by the war. But any appreciation of this character must be very tentative, since insufficient time has elapsed to estimate accurately even the immediate changes, while the situation will vary from time to time as the war proceeds. For the present purpose

attention is restricted to the categories of persons who at the outbreak of war came within the scope of the activity of the Intergovernmental Committee. No account is taken of the new classes of refugees which the war may create. Subject to these very important qualifications the more important qualifications and the more important effects of the war on the problem appear to be the following:

(a) First, there is the question of those persons inside Germany who were included within the scope of the Intergovernmental Committee. These were defined in the resolution dated July 14th 1938 as follows: "Persons who have not already left their country of origin (Greater Germany), but who must emigrate on account of their political opinions, religious beliefs or racial origin." Little authentic information is available regarding the present attitude of the German authorities towards this class. While there has not been any general invitation to Jews to return to Germany as reported in the press, it appears to be true that efforts have been made to induce individual Jews with special qualifications to return. Reports from Jewish sources are to the effect that more Jews have been taken into employment, and particularly into labor corps, but that the policy of the authorities is still to emigrate as many Jews as possible and to continue to exert pressure to this end. The Jews in Germany are very nervous about

57

their future and are anxious to emigrate if allowed to do so. They hope that some external agency will be able to assist them. This presumably would have to be a neutral organization. On the other hand, it is prima facie reasonable to assume that Germany will not wish, during a time of war, to get rid of any person who is likely to be of use in the prosecution of the war. Similarly, it may be assumed that she will still wish to get rid of persons whose emigration would assist the prosecution of the war by relieving the pressure on her economic resources or for any other reason. It may further be assumed that, given the opportunity, she would use the emigration of refugees to establish her agents in a belligerent country. If these assumptions are correct they raise at once a very important question of policy. There are five Governments now at war with Germany who are represented on the Intergovernmental Committee, namely, the United Kingdom, France, Canada, Australia and New Zealand. Will it be possible for them to continue to subscribe to an activity of the Committee which they might consider would help the enemy? In other words, will it be possible to continue to include within the scope of the Committee persons who have not already left Greater Germany, their country of origin? This, it may be observed, is a question quite distinct from the attitude which the Government of a neutral country as such may wish to adopt

towards the immigration of persons proceeding direct from
Germany, or towards such other measures as it may be
able to take in the interest of the Jews inside Germany.
This is purely the concern of the individual government,
and is distinct from the policy which the Intergovernmental
Committee, as an international body, may wish to adopt.
One of the objects of the Committee, as stated in the
Resolution dated July 14, 1938, was the following:

"To improve the present conditions of exodus of refugees from Greater Germany and to replace them by conditions of orderly emigration."

The Director, as chief executive officer of the Committee, was directed to undertake negotiations with the German authorities for the purpose of achieving this object.
So far as negotiations or discussions with the German
authorities are concerned, it would appear obvious that
these have come to an end, and cannot be resumed during
the war. So far as direct emigration of refugees from
Germany is concerned (as a function of the committee),
without attempting to anticipate the decision of the
committee on this point, it appears reasonable to assume,
for the present purpose, that it will be inconsistent
with the general policy of those Governments represented
on the Committee which are now at war with Germany.

(b) If this is so, there remains the second category

59

of persons, namely, those "who have already left their
country of origin and who have not yet established themselves permanently elsewhere." The object of the Intergovernmental Committee as stated in the Resolution above
cited was to develop opportunities of permanent settlement
for these. In short, it would appear that the practical
work of the Committee, insofar as it is not extended to
categories not at present included, will be confined to
those persons who are in countries of temporary refuge.
For the sake of conveniences such countries may be classi-
fied as (1) belligerent countries; (2) neutral European
countries; (3) neutral non-European countries.

60

    (c) The belligerent countries of temporary refuge are
the United Kingdom and France. The present policy of the
British Government towards refugees in the United Kingdom is
to regard Czech refugees as friendly aliens and German and
Austrian refugees as technically enemy aliens. There is,
however, no intention to follow a policy of general internment. While the safety of the State must be the first
consideration, and the individuals are liable to internment,
the general policy is to allow as many as can be safely
allowed to take up employment as opportunities occur, and
even to do some forms of national service. In order to
ascertain those who can be safely allowed these concessions,
a number of tribunals have been established which will

classify the refugees according to their reliability. It
is probable that as a result of this examination and the
overriding executive powers of the Government, a comparatively small number will be interned. A larger number
will be free from any restrictions, while the great
majority, while free to seek employment, will be subject
to minor restrictions, e. g. periodical reports to the
police. This, however, is merely an estimate.

It is too early to give more than an indication of how
this policy will affect the private organizations. An
uncertain factor is the attitude of the public towards
persons of German origin or nationality, even although those
persons have been the victims of German aggression. So far,
public reactions have been more favorable than might have
been anticipated. At the middle of September about 8,000
domestic servants had been dismissed from their employment
and were a charge on the private bodies. But in many cases
dismissals were due to the readjustment of households and
the closing down of establishments which were a direct
result of the war. None the less, from one fourth to one
third of the dismissals were due to the not unnatural prejudice against retaining enemy aliens in service. On the
other hand, comparatively few guarantors for the care of
children have tried to resile from their agreements, and
most of the cases that have occurred are due to a genuine

61

change in material circumstances. If public opinion remains favorable, a large number of the refugees should be absorbed in remunerative employment, but there will be a time-lag of at least several months before employment is general, and during this period the strain on the resources of the private organizations for maintenance and support will be greater than before the war. At the same time, as explained in a memorandum on a later item in the agenda, the ability of the private organizations to raise funds in England will be very greatly reduced, and possibly be almost non-existent.

It seems unlikely that the United Kingdom will be able to admit any more refugees of enemy origin.

62

(d) No official information has been received regarding the policy of the French Government towards refugees in France. It appears from private sources, however, that in the first place male Austrian and German refugees have been interned, but that their cases will be examined by Commissions, and that following this examination use will be made in various forms of employment, including national service, of those in regard to whose reliability there is no doubt. It is not known whether the French Government will desire to emigrate some of the refugees if openings and facilities are available.

(e) Little information is at present available regarding the position in European neutral countries. The three countries which have received most refugees as temporary visitors are Holland, Belgium and Switzerland. Even before the war their presence was the cause of much embarrassment to the Governments and was placing a very heavy strain on the private organizations. The common desire was to emigrate as many as possible and as quickly as possible. The war cannot fail to increase the difficulties of the Governments and of private bodies, who may be expected to urge that the emigration of refugees be pressed forward.

(f) Before the war the position of refugees in non-European countries of temporary refuge, e. g. Shanghai, was deplorable. They were dependent for support on the charity of private organizations, and the opportunities for re-emigration were small. The problem in their case will be to continue private relief and to explore permanent means of livelihood.

5. Assuming that as a function of the Committee direct emigration from Germany will cease to all intents and purposes, the problem of finding new homes is now reduced to the re-emigration of a certain number of persons from countries of temporary refuge. In paragraph 3 (b) above, an estimate is given of the number of these at the end of August 1939. The figure given is 156,000, of whom 140,000 were in European countries. It is impossible

63

to say as yet how the war will affect these. Much depends
on the policy of Great Britain and France, and the demand
for labor both during and after the war in these countries.
There is the further consideration that the object for which
Great Britain and France are fighting is to bring to an
end the system of Nazism which inter alia is the direct cause
of the refugee problem of Greater Germany. When this object
has been attained, it should be possible for many of the
Jewish refugees to resume their life in Germany.

It would therefore appear that the immediate problems
are, first, to provide for the maintenance and support of
refugees in countries of temporary refuge, and second, to
relieve the pressure on those countries by re-emigration.
(End of memorandum).

In amplification of the memorandum Sir Herbert Emerson
explained that after it was written a message was received
from the German authorities.

Sir Herbert Emerson: Referring to the discussions
with the German authorities, I wish to read a message
which was received from Mr. Wohlthot after the outbreak
of war. I think it is of importance. It reached Mr.
Achilles about the end of September, and this was the
wording:

"The Government of the German Reich is willing to
continue cooperation with the Intergovernmental Committee

with respect to the emigration of Jews from Germany. Such
emigrants will be permitted to take their effects with
them with the exception of certain articles of which there
is a shortage in Germany. Under the present circumstances
no funds in Germany may be used for the transportation of
either persons or effects beyond the German border. Property
left in Germany by Jews will be put at the disposal of the
Reich Committee for German Jews, for the support of needy
persons of that race in Germany."

So it would seem that even if the committee were
able to arrange for the direct emigration of persons from
Germany, no financial help would be forthcoming from their
own assets or wealth, except that they would be allowed
to take their personal effects with them, whatever they
may be. It would thus appear difficult in the conditions of
a war to assume that it will be still possible for the
Committee to carry on its function of direct contact.
That is, of course, a matter for the Committee to decide.
I am merely putting forth what seems to me a prima facie
difficulty.

Another function of the Committee is to find permanent
homes for those who have left Germany but are still in
countries of temporary refuge.

Whatever may be the position as regards the other
two functions, it is clear that this function remains, and

65

as I have suggested, there is a great deal of work to
be done in that direction.

There are 140,000 persons in Europe who are not assured
of permanent homes and there are about 16,000 outside of
Europe who have still no permanent means of livelihood.
There are 140,000 to be re-emigrated from European countries
of temporary refuge, and about 16,000 to be re-emigrated
from outside Europe.

There again even that part of the problem may be
simplified to some extent for the time being.

Mr. McDonald: Might I interrupt? Have you the figures
for the break down of that 140,000 in the various countries?

Sir Herbert Emerson: I am afraid I have not accurate
figures, because the 140,000 is not the total in those
countries, which is much larger. The number of 140,000
represents the persons in those countries who cannot stay
there, who have to be re-emigrated.

Count de Saint-Quentin: A few minutes before you gave
us two figures, 16,000 for the Jews outside of Europe and
147,000 for those inside Europe? I suppose they are about
the same figures?

Sir Herbert Emerson: I ought to have given you 140,000
inside Europe and 16,000 outside. These are very rough
figures, of course, only approximations.

But as I was saying, even taking that restricted part

of the problem, the war may, for the time being, simplify it to some extent. For instance, quite a number of the 140,000 I mentioned are in England and in France. I don't know the figures for France. Perhaps His Excellency may know them?

Cout de Saint-Quentin: Between forty and fifty thousand.

Sir Herbert Emerson: The figures in England at the outbreak of the war were about 50,000 altogether, of which probably something like 25,000 would have had to re-emigrate. When war broke out, the British Government decided not to intern all enemy aliens as it had done in the previous war. It interned a few who were obviously enemy agents, but for the rest, it allowed them their liberty under certain restrictions. They could not move outside a radius of 5 miles without permission, and so on. But the great majority of them it allowed to stay where they were and they were not interned.

The British Government then set up a number of tribunals presided over either by high judicial officers or by members of the bar. I think altogether there are about 110 such tribunals. The function of each tribunal is to examine the cases of about 500 enemy aliens, and those enemy aliens of course include all the refugees from Greater Germany.

67

So far as the refugees are concerned, the tribunal starts with the initial presumption that a refugee who has had to flee from Nazi persecution is a friendly alien, and if the tribunal finds that it is not necessary to intern a particular refugee, he will be allowed, subject to appeal to retain his liberty unless he does something which forfeits it. He will have an endorsement on his registration certificate saying that he is a refugee from Nazi persecution and he will be allowed to obtain work through the labor exchanges.

When we left England the tribunals had only just begun their work, and it is not possible to indicate what the result may be. But one hopes that as a result of this examination the great majority, at least 90 percent of the refugees from Greater Germany, will be allowed to retain their liberty; and futher, one hopes that within the course of the next few months the great majority of those who are at liberty will be able to obtain some form of remunerative employment. Some of them possibly will go into national service, others into various jobs that the war will create.

Lord Winterton: At this point I might just supplement what our director has said. As a member of the British Government I would like to pay testimony to the great eagerness shown by the refugees that we have in our country to serve our country in some way in time of war, and it is hoped that of this 90 percent that will be allowed to work, by far the larger number will be employed directly upon war work. Some are anxious to join a legion, if it can be formed, and I have understood that some are going to serve in the legion in your country. (Referring to France).

But I think that is right to say, because it does **really** have a bearing on the problem, it affects all of the countries represented around this table, that with the exception of perhaps 10 percent, the 90 percent remaining are anxious, **in** the very big events which are pending in Europe, to take their full share in helping the country of temporary refuge in which they find themselves at this moment. And those of us who have had experience with that, are very pleased with the attitude which they have adopted towards our country.

69

Mr. Taylor: Mr. Chairman, in that connection may I say that I was told by some of the Jewish leaders in New York last week, that 65,000 men of military age had offered their services in Palestine.

Lord Winterton: I think that is true, Mr. Taylor.

Sir Herbert Emerson: I have no official information as to what the position is in France. Perhaps his Excellency, the Ambassador, will correct me if I am wrong, but from the non-official information I have received, I understand that owing to the geographical position of France, and owing to the fact that France has very many more aliens and particularly enemy aliens than Great Britain, it was necessary at the beginning of the war to intern the able-bodied men. But there also I understand it is the intention to set up commissions similar to the tribunals in England, who will examine the cases of each of the refugees, and that once the commission has passed a refugee as reliable, he will be allowed to work, to take up remunerative employment, and perhaps also to undertake some form of national service. I think that is the position.

Count de Saint-Quentin: Yes, I touched upon it in my preliminary remarks. I must add that apparently we have concentration camps and internment camps. Of course, a concentration camp is a limited space for a limited number of people who are under strict supervision. Internment might be in villages or small towns, where the people are supposed to move within a certain radius, probably some miles, 5 miles, as you just said in England. We know that already a certain number of people have been set free, absolutely, and that the intention of our Government is to release a great number of people and to make the process quicker. I don't think that will be before tribunals, but that will be, as you just said, before some commissions.

As for work, just now, there are in the internment and concentration camps, especially in the internment camps, several hundred young people, for example, being taught respectively millinery for girls, or mechanics for men, or

70

in other places farming. So those places will easily find
employment either on the land or perhaps for mechanics
also in connection with national efforts for those people.
And there are a good many of them who have volunteered for
doing so.

Sir Herbert Emerson: Well, that is the position as regards Great Britain and France, the one may hope that as a
result of the inquiries now being made by the tribunals
in the one case and the commissions in the other, more of
those refugees will be able to support themselves in due
course than was the case immediately before the war. But
there will be necessarily a time lag. The war has upset
conditions of employment in England, and possibly also in
France, and there will be a time lag before the employment
of those refugees who are allowed to work will be given work.
In the meantime, in England at any rate, they have to be
supported by the private organizations, and the private
organizations are finding that a heavy burden.

The war had the immediate effect of throwing back
on their hands quite a number of refugees who were in
employment. For instance, in England, permanent employment had been given to a very large number of domestic
servants. When the war came a number of householders
either had to economize or the husband went to war, and the
wife had to make other arrangements. There was also perhaps,

71

not unnaturally, a prejudice among some people against employing people who spoke very little English and whose mother tongue was German. An immediate result of the war was thus to throw something like 8,000 domestic servants out of employment and make them dependent for relief and maintenance on the funds of the private organizations.

So although one may hope that after a few months the burdens on those organizations will be less than they were before the war, for the moment they are very definitely heavy.

The British organizations are now devoting all the funds at their disposal for the purpose of relief and main-tenance. Occasionally they are able to help a refugee to emigrate where he has already got his visa, but that is rare, and speaking generally the funds of the British private organizations are now being devoted to relief and maintenance.

I imagine that that is probably true also in France.

Count de Saint-Quentin: That is just the same case in France.

Sir Herbert Emerson: That is the position in the belligerent countries.

When we come to the neutral countries, the three countries that took most refugees in temporarily were Holland, Belgium, and Switzerland, although practically every country had a certain number of them. The Scandanavian countries have taken in quite a good number. Sweden, for instance,

has something between three and four thousand. Yugoslavia
has a certain number. Roumania has a certain number, and
so on. There is hardly a country in Europe that has not
a certain number of them. But the countries mainly affected
are, I think, Belgium, Holland, and Switzerland.

Holland has got about 25,000 at least; in Belgium
accurate figures are not available, but I should say that
there are at least 15,000; and Switzerland has probably
got something like 12,000.

Even before the war the situation was becoming increasingly embarrassing in those countries. In spite of
all the precautions they took, the number coming into the
countries, either legally or illegally, was considerably
in excess of the number going out by emigration. The private organizations were finding it increasingly difficult
to finance their maintenance.

In Belgium, the Government had already come to the
assistance of the private organizations and was making itself responsible for the upkeep of about 3,000 refugees,
while in the Netherlands the Government had very
generously started the building of a central camp for refugees.

Not only was the situation embarrassing to those countries financially, but there was a grave danger of anti-
Semitic feeling arising, and of a certain amount of economic

73

disturbance because the refugees were interfering to some extent with the labor market.

Here again I have no full official information about what the position now is, but from what information I have, and from my knowledge of the previous situation, I think it is safe to assume that the war will aggravate the position in those countries in several respects.

In the first place, the private organizations will find it more difficult to collect funds. In the second place, there may be - one hopes there will not be - fewer opportunities for emigration than before. And in the third place, one might expect that the governments may find the presence of a large number of persons of German origin and nationality more embarrassing in war time than they have found it in peace time. Fourthly, the war, as far as one can see, is likely to be a disturbing factor so far as economic conditions in those countries are concerned.

So although I have no precise information on the matter, I would expect that the conditions facing both the Governments of those countries and also the private organizations, would be more difficult during the war than they are before.

74

In support of that assumption, I may say that Mr. Pell
has just handed me a letter conveying a telegram from my
deputy, in which he says that he has received messages
both from the Belgian and the Swiss Governments asking
me to bring forward prominently at this conference the
urgent necessity of Emigration of refugees from those
countries.

To sum up. So far as the problem of Greater Germany
is concerned – and we all know there are likely to be
many other problems, problems of refugees from Poland
and so on, but I am not dealing with these at the moment,
I am taking merely the case of refugees from Greater
Germany – it seems that for one reason or another the
problem will be more restricted in one sense, since it
seems obvious that emigration from Greater Germany will
be on a lesser scale. It may be easier also because
in Great Britain and France, employment is likely to be
more plentiful for the refugees and the restrictions
on their taking work will be relaxed.

75

But on the other hand, in the neutral countries, the
conditions are likely to be more difficult, and moreover,
so far at any rate, as Europe is concerned, it is going to
be much more difficult for the private organizations to

obtain the funds which they have been able to secure in the past.

I might perhaps add this. So far as information has drifted through from Germany - I have no doubt many of the gentlemen present are in a much better position to give more accurate information than I am - the Jews in Germany are feeling nervous and frightened about their position, they are naturally uncertain as to what is going to happen to them, and they would, of course, welcome any opportunity for leaving Germany, that might arise.

That leads me to one point which I had omitted to mention. I think it may be assumed, certainly so far as Great Britain is concerned, and I imagine also as regards France, that while the war lasts neither of those countries will be able to take many more refugees into them.

So far as Great Britain is concerned, it has agreed to liquidate certain commitments made before the war. For instance, there were a number of Jewish refugees in Germany, Austria, and Czechoslovakia, who had been given certificates for emigration to Palestine. Provided that the authorities are satisfied that the persons presenting certificates are the persons to whom they were granted, and that they are not enemy agents, I understand that those persons will be still allowed to go to Palestine. But when that has been liquidated, I understand that it will only be in very exceptional circumstances that Great Britain will be able to admit anyone direct from Germany.

Such is the general position, as I see it, and the changes which have been created by the war. But I would like to say that this appreciation is made within a few weeks of war breaking out, and of course may be completely altered by developments.

Lord Winterton: Mr. McDonald, I think you were anxious to make a statement.

Mr. James G. McDonald: Mr. Chairman, before I make this statement on behalf of the President's Advisory Committee on Political Refugees, of which I am Chairman, I should like to say, if I may do so, that as a former commissioner dealing with the general problem of German refugees, I feel a high regard for the report which Sir Herbert has just now given us, and for the wholly admirable and energetic far-sighted leadership which he has displayed from the very time when he first took over this responsibility

And also in a preliminary way, I should like to say that those of us who are members of the President's Advisory Committee should be very happy and consider it a privilege to be of any service we can to either the Chairman of the Intergovernmental Committee, or to Sir Herbert, or to Mr. Van Zeeland, when he comes, either here in Washington or subsequently when you are in New York. In other words, if we can be of any use whatsoever in the contacts with the private organizations or supplying secretarial help, or in any other way, we should consider it a privilege to do it.

The President's Advisory Committee on Political Refugees has been pleased to cooperate with the Intergovernmental Committee with respect to its efforts to develop opportunities for permanent settlement. In pursuit of this objective it organized commissions of experts to explore the possibilities of settlement in British Guiana, the Dominican Republic, and the Philippines.

The report of the British Guiana Survey Commission has already been presented to the Intergovernmental Committee. It is possible to submit at this meeting of the officers of the Intergovernmental Committee reports on the inquiries in the Dominican Republic and in the Philippines.

The experts who visited the Dominican Republic found that the northeastern part of the island offers excellent colonization possibilities. Some 200,000 acres in this area were considered feasible for the colonization of approximately 28,500 refugee families. The report recommended an initial trial settlement of a small number of refugees and that larger numbers be introduced as experience warranted. Since the receipt of the report the President's Advisory Committee on Political Refugees has assisted negotiations between interested private groups and the representatives of the Dominican Republic. These negotiations culminated recently in a financial commitment by the private groups to make available a sum of $200,000, toward the cost of trial settlement of 500 families. A private settlement corporation is

soon to be formed to complete negotiations. The Dominican
Republic has expressed its willingness to facilitate plans
for settlement and to accept refugees in numbers found to
be practical by the experience of the trial settlement.

Perhaps I might interpolate in reference to the Dominican
project the suggestion that the Intergovernmental Committee
may find it useful to take count of this study up to date,
either by some reference to it in its communique, or otherwise. I am sure that would be appreciated by the private
groups, and I think it would also have a useful effect in
Santo Domingo.

The report of the Mindanao Exploration Commission -
the Philippine Commission centered its attention on the
Island of Mindanao - has become available more recently.
The experts determined that certain areas of the Island
of Mindanao, by reason of climate, elevation, health conditions, topography, and soil, are well adapted to European
colonization and successful agricultural development for
as many as 10,000 individuals. It passed favorably on
some 100,000 acres of land in these areas. These lands
are near existing transportation facilities and will not
require extensive building of roads. President Quezon
of the Commonwealth Government has publicly stated his
interest in the project and his willingness to cooperate in
its development. There has already been some infiltration
of refugees in the Philippine Islands and the project if

undertaken immediately will undoubtedly provide new opportunities for a livelihood for many refugees now seeking a new home. There has not been sufficient time since the receipt of the report to consider the problem of financing the settlement in the Philippines but careful estimates included in the report total $410,000.00 for the initial group of 600 settlers proposed and from $5,580,000 to $6,080,000 for the maximum of 10,000 immigrants envisaged.

I might add perhaps that at a meeting last week in New York of the President's Advisory Committee, when we had as guests certain members of the Philippine Commission, Mr. Taylor and two representatives of the State Department, it was the sense of the private groups interested at the end of the meeting that it might be practical to implement this report within a matter of weeks, rather than months, that it might be within five or six weeks that the initial financing could be arranged and the first of the pioneers, if you wish to call them such, certain engineers, workmen, agricultural leaders, might actually be on their way from, as it was hoped, some of the centers of greatest congestion of refugees today.

Lord Winterton: Does that conclude your talk?

Mr. McDonald: Yes.

Lord Winterton: I hope you will allow me to say on my own behalf, and I am sure on behalf of my colleague, how invaluable has been the aid of your Committee, quite in-

valuable to this Committee. I am sure Sir Herbert would
like to associate himself with that. We could not have gone
on at all without it. I would like to make this acknowledg-
ment of the help we have received from it.

Now Your Excellencies and gentlemen, I don't know what
your views are about the session today. It seems to me
- I haven't had the opportunity of consulting anybody on
this point - but it seems to me that the items 2, 3, and 4
and 5 would rather come together maybe for the purpose of
discussion and we had better discuss them as one, and I think
it will be difficult to enter upon that discussion this
afternoon. I think we should really devote tomorrow morning
to that discussion, although before we adjourn this afternoon I think Mr. Pell has received a communication from the
Swiss Minister.

81

Mr. Robert Pell: The Swiss Minister has notified the
Secretary of the Committee that he has received instructions
from his Government to make a statement to the officers. I
explained to him the set-up of the Committee and suggested
that perhaps he might wish to communicate his statement
through one of the officers, but he feels that he should
speak to the officers personally. I promised to submit his
request to the Chariman and the officers.

Lord Winterton: I think we don't want to stand on what
we call in our English slang, red tape. Mr. Morris, will
you, as Acting Secretary, give your advice on that? Is there

anything in the constitution of the conference that would prevent us hearing his Excellency if he should wish to come before us?

Mr. Morris: I believe there is not.

Mr. Pell: I see no reason why he should not come if the officers are agreeable to his appearing.

Señor Don Felipe A. Espil: I see no reason why we shouldn't allow him.

Mr. Pell: I don't think that there will be very many requests from governments. Naturally, private people cannot appear before us, but the Swiss Government is a member of the Committee and I suppose that they are entitled to make that request.

82

Count de Saint-Quentin: I was just wondering why the Swiss Government doesn't belong to our Committee.

Mr. Pell: They do, sir, but this group is the executive of the Committee. Thirty-two Governments belong to the Committee, and this group is the executive. It was understood that in order to facilitate the business there would be this executive, and the Swiss Minister had a perfect right to communicate his views through one of the officers. But he says that the instructions which he has received are such that he must make this request.

Count de Saint-Quentin: I should think very naturally that we should hear him.

Mr. Taylor: That is my view.

The Honorable Dr. Loudon: That is also my view.

Lord Winterton: I think there is nothing in the constitution of our conference that would prevent it, and I
think we should tell His Excellency that we should be
pleased to have him, and if it would suit him, the first
thing tomorrow morning. Will you communicate with him,
Mr. Morris?

Mr. Morris: Yes.

The Honorable Dr. Loudon: I heard Mr. McDonald speak
about the possibility of settling refugees in the Philippine
Islands.

Do you want me to present the statement on behalf of
the Government of the Netherlands now, or do you wish me to
wait until tomorrow?

Lord Winterton: I think it would be better, Your Excellency, to give it tomorrow. I have also a statement to
make about British Guiana.

I haven't had an opportunity of consulting privately
with the Vice Chairman, but it seems to me, and though
I don't want to influence the decision too much, we might
perhaps have a little private talk about it afterwards,
that it may be necessary to have a further sitting after
tomorrow. It seems to me that it will be very difficult
to get through everything tomorrow, and it might be necessary
to adjourn the meeting for a day or so.

For example, His Excellency, the French Ambassador,

83

stated I think in his remarks, that he might have to communicate with his Government, and I might have to communicate
with my Government, on the last item of the agenda. So I
would propose tomorrow to suggest formally to the conference
that if it is necessary to do so, we should adjourn to a
further date if we cannot conclude the business tomorrow.
But if any of Your Excellencies have any objections to
that, perhaps we might have a private talk about it afterwards.

Count de Saint-Quentin: I wasn't thinking of communica-
ting with my Government for special instructions, but I just
said that certain points might arise beyond my competence,
and I probably would have to simply submit suggestions or
proposals to my Government.

Lord Winterton: I wasn't asking Your Excellencies to
come to a decision now, but it seems to me that the matters
are of such importance which are raised in the President's
speech, that we should not necessarily end our proceedings
tomorrow if we could find a day mutually convenient to all
the vice chairmen when we could meet again and have the conference again.

Mr. Taylor, will you say a word on that?

Mr. Taylor: I should think that if it is necessary because of the one larger point of extending the scope of the
Committee's authority, or its right to investigate in a
field which heretofore they have not covered, that to do it

in a very direct way and have harmony of opinion among the
officers, we might very well tomorrow, if it were necessary,
adjourn until next week, Wednesday or Thursday, and have
a concluding session then. As I understand, Lord Winterton, and Sir Herbert are going to be present at that time.
What we do should be very well considered now in advance
of the action.

Lord Winterton: Exactly.

Then, Mr. Pell, what time would you suggest that we
meet tomorrow?

Mr. Pell: We would suggest 11 o'clock.

Lord Winterton: If that suits everyone, the session is
concluded until 11 tomorrow, when we will take up 2, 3, 4,
and 5 on the agenda.

85

I have to announce that the photographers who are
in the Secretary's office would like to take a photograph
of the Chairman and Vice Chairmen.

(Thereupon, an adjournment was taken at 5:10 o'clock
p.m. until the following day, Wednesday, October 18, 1939,
at 11 o'clock a.m.).

There is given here for the convenience of members
of the Committee the full text of President Roosevelt's
statement of October 17, 1938, as follows:

I am glad to welcome at the White House Lord Winterton, the Chairman; Sir Herbert Emerson, the Director; Mr. Myron Taylor, the Vice-Chairman of the Intergovernmental Committee representing the United States of America, the heads of missions of the Argentine Republic, Brazil, France and the Netherlands; and Mr. James G. McDonald, the Chairman of my Advisory Committee on Political Refugees.

I extend through you to the thirty-two Governments participating in the Intergovernmental Committee and to the private refugee organizations my appreciation for the assistance which has been given to refugees in the period since the meeting at Evian. I hope the work will be carried on with redoubled vigor, and with more positive results.

In March, 1938 it became clear to the world that a point had been reached where private agencies alone could no longer deal with the masses of unfortunate people who had been driven from their homes. These men, women and children were beating at the gate of any nation which seemed to offer them a haven.

Most of these fellow human beings belonged to the Jewish Race, though many thousands of them belonged to other races and other creeds. The flight from their countries of origin meant chaos for them and great difficulties for other nations which for other reasons -- chiefly economic -- had erected barriers against immigration. Many portions of the world which in earlier years provided areas for immigration had found it necessary to close the doors.

Therefore, a year and a half ago I took the initiative by asking thirty-two governments to cooperate with the Government of the United States in seeking a long range solution of the refugee problem. Because the United States through more than three centuries has been built in great measure by people whose dreams in other lands had been thwarted, it seemed appropriate for us to make possible the meeting at Evian, which was attended by Mr. Myron C. Taylor as my personal representative.

That meeting made permanent the present Intergovernmental Committee, and since that time this Intergovernmental Committee has greatly helped in the settling of many refugees, in providing temporary refuge for thousands of others and in making important studies toward opening up new places of final settlement in many parts of the world.

I am glad to be able to announce today that active steps have been taken to begin actual settlement, made possible by the generous attitude of the Dominican Government and the Government of the Philippine Commonwealth. This is, I hope, the forerunner of many other similar projects in other nations.

Furthermore, I am glad to note the establishment of a distinguished Anglo-American group of the Coordinating Foundation, which with the help of your Committee will investigate the suitability of other places of settlement for immigrants.

87

Things were going well, although I must confess slowly, up to the outbreak of the war in Europe. Today we must recognize that the regular and planned course of refugee work has been of necessity seriously interrupted.

The war means two things.

First, the current work must not be abandoned: It must be redirected. We have with us the problem of helping those individuals and families who are at this moment in countries of refuge and who for the sake of the world and themselves can best be placed in permanent domiciles during the actual course of the war without confusing their lot with the lot of those who in increasing numbers will suffer as a result of the war itself.

88

That I may call the short range program, and it presents a problem of comparatively small magnitude. In a moment you will see why I say, "comparatively small magnitude." At this moment there are probably not more than two or three hundred thousand refugees who are in dire need and who must as quickly as possible be given opportunity to settle in other countries where they can make permanent homes.

This is by no means an insoluble task, but it means hard work for all of us from now on -- and not only hard work but a conscientious effort to clear the decks of an old problem -- an existing problem, before the world as a whole is confronted with the new problem involving infinitely more human beings, which will confront us when the present war is over. This last is not a cheerful prospect, but it will be the almost inevitable result of present conflicts.

That is why I specifically urge that this Intergovernmental Committee redouble its efforts. I realize, of course, that Great Britain and France, engaged as they are in a major war, can be asked by those nations which are neutral to do little more than to give a continuance of their sympathy and interest in these days which are so difficult for them. That means that upon the neutral nations there lies an obligation to humanity to carry on the work.

I have suggested that the current task is small in comparison with the future task. The war will come to an end some day; and those of us who are realists know that in its wake the world will face a refugee problem of different character and of infinitely greater magnitude.

Nearly every great war leaves behind it vast numbers of human beings whose roots have been literally torn up. Inevitably there are great numbers of individuals who have lost all family ties -- individuals who find no home to return to, no occupation to resume -- individuals who for many different reasons must seek to rebuild their lives under new environments.

Every war leaves behind it tens of thousands of families who for very many different reasons are compelled to start life anew in other lands.

89

Economic considerations may affect thousands of families and individuals.

All we can do is to estimate on the reasonable doctrine of chances, that when this ghastly war ends there may be not one million but ten million or twenty million men, women and children belonging to many races and many religions, living in many countries and possibly on several continents, who will enter into the wide picture -- the problem of the human refugee.

I ask, therefore, that as the second great task that lies before this Committee, it start at this time a serious and probably a fairly expansive effort to survey and study definitely and scientifically this geographical and economic problem of resettling several million people in new areas of the earth's surface.

We have been working, up to now, on too small a scale, and we have failed to apply modern engineering to our task. We know already that there are many comparatively vacant spaces on the earth's surface where from the point of view of climate and natural resources European settlers can live permanently.

Some of these lands have no means of access; some of them require irrigation; most of them require soil and health surveys; all of them present in the process of settlement, economic problems which must be tied in with the economy of existing settled areas.

The possible field of new settlements covers many portions of the African, American and Australasian portions of the globe. It covers millions of square miles situated in comparatively young republics and in colonial possessions or dominions of older nations.

Most of these territories which are inherently susceptible of colonization by those who perforce seek new homes, cannot be developed without at least two or three years of engineering and economic studies. It is neither wise nor fair to send any colonists to them until the engineering and economic surveys have resulted in practical and definite plans.

91

We hope and we trust that existing wars will terminate quickly; and if that is our hope there is all the more reason for all of us to make ready, beginning today, for the solution of the problem of the refugee. The quicker we begin the undertaking and the quicker we bring it to a reasonable decision, the quicker will we be able to say that we can contribute something to the establishment of world peace.

Gentlemen, that is a challenge to the Intergovernmental Committee -- it is a duty because of the pressure of need -- it is an opportunity because it gives a chance to take part in the building of new communities for those who need them. Out of the dregs of present disaster we can distill some real achievements in human progress.

This problem involves no one race group -- no one religious faith. It is the problem of all groups and all faiths. It is not enough to indulge in horrified humanitarianism, empty resolutions, golden rhetoric and pious words. We must face it actively if the democratic principle based on respect and human dignity is to survive -- if world order, which rests on security of the individual, is to be restored.

Remembering the words written on the Statue of Liberty, let us lift a lamp beside new golden doors and build new refuges for the tired, for the poor, for the huddled masses yearning to be free.

92

CONFERENCE OF OFFICERS

of the

INTER-GOVERNMENTAL COMMITTEE ON POLITICAL REFUGEES

State Department,
Washington, D. C.

October 18, 1939 - 11 a.m.

- - - - - -

PRESENT: 93

(Same as noted for the October 17, 1939 meeting
except:

Hon. Cordell, Secretary of State - Not Present

Dr. Carl Bruggmann, Minister of Switzerland - Present

- - - - - -

Lord Winterton: We will first hear from the Minister from Switzerland, Dr. Carl Bruggmann.

The Honorable Dr. Carl Bruggmann (Switzerland): Gentlemen, I thank you for giving me the opportunity to explain in a few words the problems for Switzerland created by the refugees. There are actually between 10 and 12,000 emigrants in Switzerland. Of those, about 3000 are without any means, and must be supported by Swiss organizations. The monthly amount spent on their behalf is about 300,000 Swiss francs (about 66,000 dollars).

Unfortunately, circumstances do by no means allow the possibility to give employment to these refugees in Switzerland, nor is it possible to proceed with the readaptation of their profession. The structure of Swiss economics, particularly the fact that there are still large numbers of unemployed Swiss citizens is prohibitive. As the number of Swiss unemployed is now increased by the evacuation of Swiss citizens from various European countries, there is absolutely no hope that the circumstances in this respect might be changed in favor of the refugees. I beg leave to recall that the number of foreigners already employed in Switzerland, which is between 8 and 10 percent, is probably higher than in any other country. The situation which is often criticized even in normal times, is that about 500,000 Swiss citizens must live abroad because of not being able to find employment in their own country. In war time, the

question of food supplies will aggravate the problem. Bad
economic conditions are a good ground for bad seed. It
must be feared that the waves of foreign propaganda might
provoke feelings in my country which so far have been strange
to the big majority of our population.

It must therefore be wished from the Swiss point of
view as well as from the point of view of the refugees, who
must lead an idle life in Switzerland, to give them as soon
as possible the opportunity to settle in other countries.
It would for instance be a great help if the unexhausted
American quota for German citizens in Germany could be used
for the German refugees in Switzerland.

I am certainly permitted to make the statement that
Switzerland has never before evaded her duties to humanity
and that she is not doing so at present but owing to conditions which are imperative, refugees can only be kept in
Switzerland temporarily. They can only be helped and be
given rest and strength for their further immigration.

My Government would be very much obliged to your
committee to take these facts into consideration.

Lord Winterton: Do any of your Excellencies wish to
speak on the statement of the Swiss Minister?

Mr. Taylor: Mr. Chairman, I have listened with great
interest to the declaration by the Minister from Switzerland as to the difficulties encountered by that country due
to the fact that they have so large a number of refugees.

I am sure that the representatives of the other countries present have similar stories to tell, and may I say that these countries deserve the highest commendation for their generous offer for the reception of the refugees and hospitality to them during the period of immediate necessity.

I think the meeting will agree with President Roosevelt that our short range program should be emigration of people from those countries as soon as practical to places of final settlement. No time should be lost in tackling these problems and intensifying our efforts to relieve that acute situation.

96

I believe that the meeting will agree that the cure will have to be found partly through the process of infiltration, and partly by the program with which we are ready to go forward in the opening up of new areas of settlement.

I am sure I voice the unanimous opinion of the meeting when I say how deeply impressed we were to hear from Mr. McDonald that the technical preparations had been completed with regard to the Dominican and Philippine projects, that financing of them is being undertaken, and that the settlements, trial settlements, will be set up in both places in the near future.

Lord Winterton: Your Excellencies, I would like to associate myself on behalf of the United Kingdom Government with everything that Mr. Taylor has said. We are very much aware of the great efforts on behalf of refugees that have been made by the Swiss Government and also by the Governments of the Netherlands and Belgium, and we would wish to do everything we can to relieve them, to assist in relieving them of the great pressure that exists at the present owing to the very large number of refugees who were considered to be in transit and are now in their countries at the present time.

The Honorable Dr. Loudon: Yesterday I alluded to this point, but the speech of the Swiss Minister forces me to call your attention again to the declarations that have been made by Mr. Beucker-Andreae at the initial conference at Evian.

You yourself, Mr. Chairman, alluded to 25,000 refugees in my country. This is an enormous number, especially if the population of the Netherlands, as compared, for instance, with that of the United Kingdom, is taken into consideration. The United Kingdom has felt very strongly and something should be done, and that these refugees must be cared for. Consequently, that necessity is felt just as strongly, if not more strongly, by the Netherlands Government. These refugees, like in Switzerland, work on our employment market in a very unsatisfactory way. They give rise to all kinds of difficulties which I need not state any further, and the Netherlands feel very keenly that something has to be done, as soon as possible.

Mr. McDonald has already alluded to the examination

of the possibilities of settlement in the Philippines and
in the Dominican Republic, and, in the course of discussions
in this Committee, it has been said that other parts of the
world, especially various countries and territories overseas, might perhaps receive a certain number of refugees.
As the members of the Committee have been informed, a
commission, in close cooperation with the Netherlands Government, is investigating the prospects of settlement in
Surinam, or what is called the Netherlands Guiana.

According to information which I have just received
from my Government by telegraph, this commission has not
yet finished its examination of the question whether or not
it should be possible to settle refugees in this
Netherlands territory. However, I have been informed that
the preliminary results of the commission's study shows
that the possibilities of settlement, if any, would be very
limited.

This has to do, I think, with number 2 of the agenda.
This is the communication which my Government has asked me
to hand to this Committee.

In the course of the other points coming up, I will
make a few more observations.

Lord Winterton: Does anyone wish to speak on the
Swiss Minister's declaration?

Lord Winterton: Mr. Minister, we are extremely grateful to you for coming before us today.

(The Swiss Minister retired from the conference)

Lord Winterton: Well, gentlemen, as we agreed yesterday, we will next take up a discussion of items 2, 3, 4,
and 5 of the agenda.

I have a short statement to make on the settlement in
British Guiana on behalf of my Government. It has occurred
to me that we were unanimously of the opinion yesterday that
we should have another meeting of the Committee next week;
that meanwhile, on certain aspects of settlement, it might
be desirable for further private conferences to be held
between Sir Herbert Emerson and Mr. McDonald, as representing
the American refugee organizations, and it may be possible
at some time next week to have more detailed information
on certain aspects, on certain of the schemes.

Perhaps I might make an announcement, if I may, about
British Guiana at the start. It comes within item 2 of the
agenda.

My Government has instructed me to make the following
statement:

With regard to the scheme for the settlement of refugees
in British Guiana, the position is that the private organizations sponsoring this scheme were unable to proceed
with the proposed two-year experimental settlement, owing
to the outbreak of the war, and it must therefore be
regarded as indefinitely suspended.

With regard to the assistance promised by Her Majesty's Government in the form of the provision of arterial communications (should the experimental settlement and the investigation of industrial possibilities indicate that large scale settlement was practicable) this must now of necessity be ruled out at any rate for the duration of the war. If, however, the necessary funds could be secured from other sources, and no financial obligation fell upon Her Majesty's Government, or the Government of the Colony, Her Majesty's Government would give all facilities for the initiation of an experimental settlement on the lines originally contemplated. Pending the outcome of the Washington deliberations, consideration of other schemes for the development of the Colony would be deferred by the Colonial Office.

The reference in the last paragraph is to certain schemes which I understand have been put forward, not necessarily connected with the refugee settlement, by certain persons, and my Government has informed those persons or organizations that they could not consider those schemes until a decision had been reached on the subject of refugee settlement in British Guiana.

Perhaps I might add to these instructions by saying that naturally my Government regrets that it cannot any longer supply the funds which will be necessary for these arterial roads and other things, and I believe equally the

100

private refugee organizations in Great Britain - Sir Herbert Emerson is in closer touch with them than I am - must regret that they cannot find the money, for the reasons made in my speech yesterday.

Sir Herbert Emerson: I might perhaps just explain that previous to the war a British Guiana corporation was about to be set up for the purpose of carrying on the settlement in British Guiana, and in particular for financing the experimental stage.

Negotiations with the Colonial Office were almost complete when the war came. On the British side, some of the organizations had agreed to put up a certain amount of money and on the American side other American organizations had agreed to put up at least an equal sum and probably a larger sum.

When the war came, the private organizations in England were unable to guarantee the money which had been previously promised, and I understand that in those circumstances one, at any rate, of the American organizations has also asked to be absolved from their previous promise. That is the position at the moment.

But, as Lord Winterton has said, if the money was forthcoming from private sources, the British Government would be quite prepared to do what they could, in making land available in the colonies. That is the position at the moment.

Lord Winterton: Yes, it is a little more definite than that, I have more definite instruction to say that we should be prepared to offer all the facilities, including land, apart from financial aid.

Sir Herbert Emerson: But there is at the moment, I think, practically no prospect of any of the British organizations being able to put up the money.

Lord Winterton: Mr. Taylor, would you support my suggestion? I merely put it forward as a suggestion that there should be private discussions between Mr. McDonald and Sir Herbert to see if anything can be effected?

102

Mr. Taylor: I would like to make that suggestion. I think this is a wonderful opportunity for the Advisory Committee and the private organizations which take such an active part in this whole matter in this country. And Sir Herbert Emerson particularly I think it would be very helpful when we get to New York for you to do that.

Sir Herbert Emerson: I am looking forward greatly to making that contact. I am particularly interested in what Mr. McDonald said about the Dominican Republic, and about the Philippines. It seems to me a very big step forward will be made if those two schemes, or even one of them, can now be translated to the stage of practical settlement, even if to begin with it is on a purely pioneering and experimental scale.

Mr. Taylor: I would think that the Dominican one was the most desirable to put in operation.

Mr. Warren: It is a little farther along.

Mr. Taylor: That is what I meant, and I think the plan of the settlement is a little more discussable than that of the Philippines.

The Honorable Dr. Loudon: I would like to ask a question. Are we going to be informed in some way about the outcome of investigations such as have been made in the Philippines and in the Dominican Republic and in British Guiana, in order that our Governments may learn on what basis it is considered possible to settle refugees in these countries? The reasons which lead to the conclusion that settlement in those countries is possible will probably be of great importance for the Dutch Government to know, especially with regard to settlement in Surinam, or Dutch Guiana, and if we only hear now that it is possible, that would not be sufficient. We should know more about it. We have in Surinam almost the same climatic conditions.

Mr. Taylor: Mr. Chairman, I think it is in order to say that for the confidential use of the Vice Chairmen and the officers of the Intergovernmental Committee, those reports are available, and it will be my suggestion that they have access to the Dominican report which has been completed for some time. The Philippine report has only

103

been completed recently, I know. I went to a dinner with Mr. McDonald and Mr. Warren in New York one night last week, and heard a report by the members of the commission.

Is there any objection to the Vice Chairmen having access to those reports, Mr. Chairman?

Lord Winterton: No, Mr. Taylor, I think it would be very right that they should. In the case of British Guiana, that report, I think, was made available.

Sir Herbert Emerson: The British Guiana report has already been made available.

The Honorable Dr. Loudon: I don't know whether the report has reached my Government.

104

Of course, what I have said at the beginning of the meeting as well as just now refers to the preliminary results of the investigation only.

Sir Herbert Emerson: I think you may take it that the members of your commission must have certainly seen the British Guiana report. The position as regards the Dominican report is that the original report was not published, as the Government of the Dominican Republic wished it to be revised or edited in some respects. I think the editing is just about completed.

Mr. Warren: The editing has only recently been made, and it hasn't been practical as yet to reprint the report. There are certain deletions and amendments that are now acceptable to the Dominican Government.

Sir Herbert Emerson: I was just wondering whether
the Dominican Government would like the report to be circulated in a corrected form for the confidential information
of the Committee.

Mr. Warren: It should be circulated only in confidence.

Sir Herbert Emerson: It seems to be that the cause
of the Dominican Government should be obtained even to the
confidential circulation of the report in a corrected form.
It would be a pity to do anything unacceptable to the
Dominican Government when it has been so liberal in placing
facilities at the disposal of the investigating commission.

Mr. Taylor: I think it is only fair to the private
organizations to say that they financed entirely the
Dominican and Philippine reports, and I think very largely
the British Guiana report, and there was a time when they
felt that they had control over the issuance of those reports
and wanted to have some information as to where they were
going before they were issued

Mr. McDonald: I recall that, but I think there would
be no difficulty in getting their consent to the distribution
of these reports.

105

Mr. Taylor: Not in this case, but there is still the
desire to have the substance of the reports kept in confidence among the officers of the Intergovermental Committee.

Sir Herbert Emerson: I think they certainly ought to
have the reports. I have given the reasons why these
reports have not been circulated, and I think the
Philippine report is only just ready.

Mr. Warren: I don't believe the Philippine Government
has yet seen it in its printed form. We would have to
check that first.

106

The Honorable Dr. Loudon: The Philippine report will
undoubtedly be very important for the Netherlands and I
suggest that it be circulated.

Lord Winterton: Might I address a question to Mr.
Taylor, the American delegation and the State Department?

I think we all of us, the delegations around this
table, feel that your Government, or rather private
organizations of this country, have taken a most prominent
part, to which I just referred, in this investigation, and
therefore it is right that we should have a very strong
regard for the opinion which you might express on this point.

Would you hold the view, which I think certainly would
be the view of my Government, that we should agree,
assuming these settlement schemes can be carried out, which
we hope will be the case within the next few months, that

first regard should be had to the position of the very
large number of refugees in countries like Switzerland,
Holland and Belgium? So far as we are concerned in the
United Kingdom, as I indicated yesterday, I don't think
I gave the figures, but I think we have something like
40,000 refugees in England at this time --

Sir Herbert Emerson: (interposing) I think it is
about 50,000.

Lord Winterton: And my Government, as was stated by
Sir Herbert yesterday, has believed that at any rate during
the war it will be possible to find employment for the
greater number of those people, and therefore the pressure
upon us is not nearly as great as it is upon the neutral
countries.

I don't know what the position of the French Government
is in this matter, whether they would desire to avail themselves of any opportunities of settlement to reduce the number of refugees in their country, or whether they would be
prepared as we are prepared to do in the case of our
refugees, to retain them.

I will say that I ought to make it clear that I realize
our position is very different from that of France, because
you have a larger number of refugees, generally, than we
have.

His Excellency Count de Saint-Quentin: The information
that I got from my Government this morning shows that we

107

have about 60,000 German and Austrian Jewish refugees. I
am told also that we have a Committee which is meeting
every week and is doing about the work which your tribunals
do, investigating and releasing a certain number of people.
It intends to set them to work, but of course that work
is rather slow because we must take into account the detail
of giving adequate occupation to those people, and take
consideration of the economic possibilities and the feelings
of the population.

So I think that we are prepared to give any of those
people who want to go to overseas countries permission to
do so, and I feel that we would welcome that possibility.

108

Mr. Taylor: I think yesterday, in my remarks, I
expressed the feeling that our short range activity should
take into account the position of Belgium, Holland, and
Switzerland, with a view to relieving the pressure in those
countries. That is the position of our government.

Lord Winterton: I think we are all in agreement around
the table on that point.

Mr. McDonald: I might, though not a member of the committee, say that the private organizations which are responsible for carrying out the settlement schemes have
clearly in mind the point which was made by the
representative of Holland.

As a matter of fact, at the meeting in New York last
Thursday, when the President's Advisory Committee met with

the Exploration Committee for the Philippines, the point
was strongly put that if it were at all practicable it would
be desirable to utilize from those three countries at the
earliest possible moment, refugees who might be available
for this project.

I merely wanted to point out that private organizations
are fully cognizant of the need and are in agreement with
the desirability of meeting that need at the earliest
possible moment.

Lord Winterton: I venture to say that that is a very
satisfactory situation. We are all in agreement on that
point, and possibly when we meet next week it may be
possible to make more definite announcements on the subject
of these schemes as a result -- Mr. McDonald, perhaps I
might break off and say that while you were out of the
room I suggested and I think Mr. Taylor and the other
delegates were in agreement, that we might utilize the next
few days before the meeting of the conference next week,
for private discussions between you and Sir Herbert on the
subject of these settlement schemes.

Mr. McDonald: Yes, I had mentioned to Sir Herbert
yesterday that I hoped he would be available in New York
for informal, private conferences with the men who are
directly responsible for these schemes, and that, as I
think he stated, fitted perfectly into his own ideas.

Sir Herbert Emerson: I certainly contemplate that, and hope we shall have the opportunity and will be able to fix up dates and time.

Mr. McDonald: The people are all there, and you can begin as soon as you get to New York.

His Excellency Count de Saint-Quentin: May I ask one question? I understand we are all in agreement, but I don't know exactly on what point.

(Laughter).

Do I understand that we are in agreement that Switzerland, Belgium and the Netherlands, because of the pressure of the refugees, should have a prior choice as to settlement of refugees? In that case, with, say, 30 or 40 thousand refugees, that would probably not exhaust them for the next two or three years.

Lord Winterton: I must take the blame for not making the position clearer. I suggested that we were in agreement that prior consideration should be given to the claims of these three countries where the number of refugees is proportionately larger, I think, of the refugees that come within our category, than that of any other countries represented on the Committee.

As to whether or not, if all of those refugees were to be moved, the available places for the next two or three years for settlement would be taken up, I wouldn't like to express an opinion.

On the basis of the last year's work, I would say that
we should be able to move them rather more quickly than that,
assuming that the quota in the United States still will
remain, which we have had in the past.

Sir Herbert could give some information on that. How
many people moved out of Europe last year?

Sir Herbert Emerson: I cannot say off-hand how many
moved out of Europe. I think the number that moved out of
Germany was at least 150,000, and it might have been as much
as 170,000.

I think all that you were contemplating, sir, was that
as far as the private organizations responsible for carrying
on these settlement schemes in the Philippines and The
Dominican Republic were concerned, that they would pay
regard to the conditions in Belgium, Holland and Switzerland,
and indeed in other countries of refuge - they are not the
only countries, Scandinavia has quite a number of refugees
also - in carrying out their settlement schemes.

But I don't think it would be within the competence of
this Committee to pass any formal resolution to that effect
which would bind the private organizations in regard to the
classes of refugees they may wish to settle in particular
countries. And if I may say so, I think any formal resolution of that kind might lead to difficulties. Conditions
may arise in which the plight of persons in Germany may be
very bad indeed, and some of them may be able to get out of

111

Germany, and I don't think any private organization would wish to pass a resolution ruling such people out of account. I think they would probably find themselves in difficulties if they did.

I think all that is contemplated is that in the present circumstances we know that there are in certain countries of temporary refuge a large number of people who are not able to work, who are a great embarrassment to their Governments, and who may at the present time, under war conditions, be more easily removed to countries of permanent settlement, than other refugees, and that we would appreciate the fact, if private organizations in carrying out their settlement schemes, could pay special regard to the difficulties of those countries.

Mr. Taylor: Mr. Chairman, I don't recall that any words were used that might be interpreted to apply exclusively to Holland, Belgium and Switzerland.

Sir Herbert Emerson: That, I think, we want to avoid.

Mr. Taylor: I think we should not give the impression here that that is our intention.

Sir Herbert Emerson: No.

Mr. Taylor: Because that might be a violation of our mandate and it might be very unfair, as Sir Herbert says, to others who may be in distress.

Sir Herbert Emerson: I was thinking of the position of the private organizations who had to carry out the schemes.

Lord Winterton: I think perhaps my phrase "prior consideration" was not a very happy one. I wasn't suggesting we should pass a resolution, but I think we have in mind that we hope that private organizations in considering these settlement schemes would pay particular regard to the position in these smaller neutral countries where there are a large number of refugees. I think that that would meet with all of our approval.

Mr. Taylor: I think so.

Sir Herbert Emerson: That is really the position.

Lord Winterton: Ambassador, does that clear it up?

His Excellency Count de Saint-Quentin: Completely. May I ask one more question. I suppose there are a good many refugees in those countries, Belgium, Switzerland, the Netherlands, France, United Kingdom, who are already on the list for coming to this country, and I don't doubt but what they must prefer to come to the United States than to Mindanao, or the Dominican Republic.

Mr. Taylor: That is true, and whenever they are reached, they will be received here, but they have to wait their turn.

His Excellency Count de Saint-Quentin: Yes. Can you tell me approximately how long in advance is that list booked, whether those people will have to wait one or two or three years?

Mr. Taylor: I don't know whether any one has the answer to that. I am informed by Mr. Moffat that there is no guaranty, that each case will be considered on its merits as the time comes.

Sir Herbert Emerson: I think the emigration is going on continuously.

His Excellency Count de Saint-Quentin: I may be wrong, but I thought you had a general list of applications from which you took every year a certain number, so that the people at the bottom of the list had to wait one or two years.

Mr. Taylor: It is safe to say that the list as it stands today will require several years to be exhausted.

Mr. Pell: You understand, Mr. Ambassador, that the German quota applies to people who, a great many of them, are in France at the present time. They are leaving all the time.

His Excellency Count de Saint-Quentin: That work is progressing?

Mr. Pell: That work is proceeding.

Mr. McDonald: As I understand the quota numbers are assigned all over the world, and if everyone uses his quota number, then for instance if the people coming out of Germany continued at the same rate as before the war, then persons who had quota numbers in England or France or elsewhere would be reached relatively less soon; but if the people who have quota numbers in Germany are not able to use them for one reason or another because of money difficulties or otherwise, then presumably other portions of the world would receive

114

additional quota numbers sooner. So that it would not be possible for the department to indicate at what point any one individual would be reached on the list. Is that right?

Mr. Pell: That is my understanding.

Mr. McDonald: That is, in proportion as the flow of emigrants, with quota numbers from Germany lessens, then the flow from other parts of the world would be proportionately increased, do you see?

His Excellency Count de Saint-Quentin: Yes.

Sir Herbert Emerson: If I may illustrate. What I understand to be the position in Great Britain, where there are certain refugees from Germany, whose quota numbers are being reached. Previous to the war - when the quota number of a refugee was reached, he had to leave Great Britain. Now I understand the policy is that he can leave or not, as he likes. No compulsion is going to be brought upon him to use his quota number and leave. But on the other hand, if he chooses to stay in England, rather than take his opportunity of going to the United States, that will imply no promise on the part of the British Government that he will be allowed to settle permanently in England. And it is possible that some of them will be willing to take their chances, and instead of using their quota to go to America, they may prefer to stay in England, at any rate for the duration of the war. That would relieve the pressure on the list.

115

On the other hand, there are a certain number leaving
every week, I think, or at any rate every month, for America
from England.

Mr. Taylor: That condition exists in the other countries that we have just named, including the Netherlands.

Sir Herbert Emerson: Yes.

Mr. Taylor: It would seem, Mr. Chairman, that our
short range program is, except for those modifications which
the war automatically imposes upon the activities of the
Director, the same as it was before, and requires no resolution or formal action by the meeting, and it would seem to
me, as you have said, that we are in agreement on the continuance, within the limits that conditions impose upon us,
of our previous activities.

Sir Herbert Emerson: I made rather a distinction between the activities of the private organizations and the
Committee. It will really be the private organizations who
will carry out the settlement schemes and it will be they
who will select the immigrants.

Lord Winterton: That, of course, is so, but we mustn't
forget that it is one of the objects in the formation of
the Committee to endeavor to find places of settlement.

Sir Herbert Emerson: I was thinking of the origin of
the emigrants. What I had in mind was that from a practical
point of view private organizations might be in a position
to take refugees from anywhere, including a certain number
who might be able to get out of Germany.

Lord Winterton: I think we are really in agreement -
I agree with Mr. Taylor, I think we really needn't linger
any longer on this Item 2 of the agenda. The position is
very much the same as it was when we met in June, subject
to the qualification, the changes, brought about by the war.

Should we then pass - I suggested that we should take
these four items together. We haven't in fact discussed
item 3, and we might pass specifically to that.

It is:

"The question of whether or not the possibilities for
individual immigration and either group or mass settlements
so far developed are adequate to meet the problem".

I suppose really the answer to that is a somewhat short
one, that we haven't got at this moment any more schemes of
settlement, mass settlement, than we had at the time of the
time of the June meeting. I don't think we could very well
have had because I think we were handling just as much as
we could do then with these various schemes in The Dominican
Republic and elsewhere, and in regard to individual
emigration, that is a question for the various countries,
not only those represented on this committee, but other
countries as well.

Do you have any statement to make on that item, Mr.
Taylor?

Mr. Taylor: My feeling is that we will continue to
explore and develop places for settlement as if the war had

not occurred, but of course subject to such conditions as the existence of war imposes upon us; and that there is no more than we can do about that item at the present moment. We are back where we were, and we will continue to make efforts to find places of settlement, and encourage the private organizations to do the same.

Sir Herbert Emerson: I think we appear to be definitely more advanced as regards to the Philippines and also, I gather, as regards settlement in the Dominican Republic. At our meeting in July we had no definite information, really, about the Philippines, and The Dominican Republic was still in the preliminary stage. I rather gather that possibly those schemes are now well within the bounds of practical experimental settlement.

Mr. Taylor: In discussing Item 3, we have in reality discussed Item 4 also, haven't we? There are no other schemes for mass settlement that I am aware of at the moment than those which we have already mentioned.

Sir Herbert Emerson: From time to time, possibilities have been mentioned of fairly large scale settlement in Ecuador, but I don't know how far they proceeded on this side.

Mr. McDonald: I may say, as far as Ecuador is concerned, that those projects were much discussed at the time when I was High Commissioner, back 3 or 4 and even 5 years ago, yes, 5 years ago. But to the private organizations

which have the responsibility, have had the responsibility,
of financing and directing these settlement schemes, Ecuador
has, for one reason or another, never made any very considerable appeal - no reflection upon the Ecuadorian Government, of course - but the difficulties inherent in settling
any considerable number of people in Ecuador have seemed to
the private organizations to be insuperable at the present
time.

Lord Winterton: And as you say, Mr. Taylor, I don't
think there are any fresh schemes for consideration by this
conference.

Mr. Taylor: I know of none.

119

Lord Winterton: Shall we pass to item 5, the problem
of financing immigration and settlement, including the
possibilities of Government participation. My Government
authorized me to make in June, and a similar statement was
made by the Prime Minister, our Prime Minister, in the House
of Commons, a statement to this effect:

"His Majesty's Government in the United Kingdom have
given very careful consideration to the serious situation
which has come about. It is clearly necessary that large
sums should be raised for the emigration of refugees but
in existing circumstances it is impossible for the private
organizations to find these sums in the measure requisite
for a satisfactory solution of the problem. His Majesty's
Government in the United Kingdom have, therefore, reached the

conclusion that unless the work of the committee is to be seriously obstructed and the countries of refuge are to be left with large numbers of refugees who cannot be absorbed, it will be necessary to depart from the principle agreed unanimously at Evian, that no participating government would give direct financial assistance to refugees.

"His Majesty's Government are, for their part, examining the manner and extent to which private subscription to an international fund to assist in defraying the expenses of overseas emigration of refugees, might be encouraged by Government participation, possibly on a basis proportionate to the amount of private subscription, and I would earnestly invite my colleagues to lay these considerations before their Governments, and to communicate their views to me without delay. If other Governments are prepared to agree to this change in principle, and to cooperate in such participation, His Majesty's Government in the United Kingdom will take the initiative in proposing a scheme for the purpose."

Well, we had answers, the Secretary of the Committee had answers, I think from two Governments. Do you remember, Sir Herbert? At any rate, it was certainly from the Norwegian Government, and I think there was one other.

The Norwegian Government expressed itself as favorable in principle to the proposal but for reasons that I mentioned yesterday, my Government can no longer maintain that offer because of the financial needs of the war.

Mr. Taylor: I think the President touched on that in his remarks yesterday.

Lord Winterton: Yes, he did.

His Excellency Count de Saint-Quentin: The French Government is in the same position as the British Government, owing to our financial needs incident to the war.

Mr. Taylor: To discuss Governmental action is to assume, as you know, in this country, what Congress would do with such a question - and that, nobody knows. Therefore, it would be most unwise for anyone to undertake to speak with any assurance or authority on that subject.

The Honorable Dr. Loudon: With regard to item 5 of the agenda, I understand that the Netherlands Government has not yet given its reply to the question which was raised at the July meeting of the Committee. I have now been instructed to inform you that the Netherlands Government must raise objections to any suggestions that the Intergovernmental Committee should abandon the adopted principle that immigration and settlement are to be financed from private sources only.

One of the arguments in corroboration of my Government's standpoint is that, should this principle be abandoned, such decision might have the effect that certain countries would be encouraged to cause the Committee's task to be extended to groups of their population. As my Government considers

121

such an extension of the Committee's activities undesirable, it wishes to see the policy of financing from private sources maintained.

On the other hand, the Netherlands Government is in principle not opposed to a moderate financial participation, but only if the following conditions are complied with:

1. Germany itself should participate financially;

2. Besides the Netherlands, other smaller countries taking part in the work started by the Evian Conference should participate financially;

3. Governmental participation should be conditioned on the extent in which assistance from private sources is given and will continue to be given.

122

The Netherlands Government, though declaring itself prepared to participate on the above basis, will not be in a position to state its definite standpoint until a concrete plan has been submitted to it.

Lord Winterton: I am in agreement with what Mr. Taylor said. I am, of course, only quoting the agenda which was prepared for this conference by the United States Government, and I think we may take it that the possibility of Government participation need not be further discussed at this meeting because the original offer which the British Government made, to be prepared to participate if certain conditions were fulfilled, no longer holds good because of the war. The French Government is in agreement with that.

True, Mr. Taylor has expressed the opinion which, if you will allow me to say so, no one could quarrel with, that it would be impossible at this period for anyone from this Government to commit Congress. Therefore, I think we need not discuss this matter further.

We have just heard an interesting discussion from our colleague from the Netherlands, but the conditions referred to in the instructions which he received do not now really arise.

I would suggest, gentlemen, if you will agree, that it would be interesting to hear from Mr. McDonald as to what the possibilities are of how the problem of financing the emigration and settlement stands at the present time, as far as his Committee is concerned, and also from Sir Herbert Emerson.

123

Mr. McDonald: Perhaps it would be better if Sir Herbert spoke first, because he has laid down certain general principles in recent public statements, which have very much impressed the private organizations in this country, and if he would reiterate those principles, then perhaps I might supplement his statement.

Sir Herbert Emerson: I have written a memorandum on the financial side of the problem (item 5 of the agenda) and this memorandum will be available for the officers (page 119 infra). Meanwhile I may give the gist of it.

The position before the war was that with one or two exceptions, the burden of financing, the maintenance, emigration of refugees, and all other expenses, had fallen on the private organizations. I made an estimate of what assistance had been received from private sources, both in money and in kind, and I estimated that up to the middle of July, 1939, private sources had contributed at least 10 million pounds in cash, and about 5 million pounds in kind.

The private organizations were already feeling the strain very severely. While there was no real diminution in the amount of money they were receiving -- in fact, in some respects they were collecting larger sums than they had previously done -- on the other hand, their expenditure was continuously increasing, and it was increasing at a greater rate. The chief reason for that was contained in the figures I gave yesterday, that although 400,000 people left Germany since 1933, nearly 160,000 of them had still not found permanent homes or any permanent means of livelihood, and as a result the private organizations were called upon to an increasing extent to provide the maintenance for these people, and were unable in addition to provide the means necessary to emigrate.

That was the position before the war, and it was because of the increasing difficulties with which the private organizations were confronted that the proposal was put forward in the July session by the representative of His Majesty's Government in the United Kingdom that some form of

governmental assistance should be devised. The basic
principle of that assistance was that it should be proportionate to the amount subscribed from private sources
and that it should be devoted to the specific purpose of
emigration.

As the Chairman has said, the war has, of course,
altered all that, and perhaps I may now read out what I
have written in the memorandum about the effect of the war
on the financing of emigration and settlement.

I say:

"It is understood that in view of the war His Majesty's
Government in the United Kingdom find it impossible to contemplate any new financial commitments which are not directly
related to its prosecution, and that therefore they can not
usefully proceed at present with the formulation of the
scheme for financial assistance mentioned in the statement
of the Right Honorable the Earl Winterton, M.P., which I
reproduced in my memorandum. On the other hand, so far as
refugees in England are concerned, it is hoped that the
liberal policy adopted by the British Government will result in many of them becoming self-supporting, and will
thus afford relief to the private organizations. In so far
as it may be necessary to intern a certain number, they
would be a charge on the State – and the same is presumably
true of those that will be interned in France, I take it
that if the State interns them, the State makes itself

125

responsible for their maintenance.

With regard to the trust fund which was formed for the relief of refugees from Czechoslovakia, it is understood that that fund will continue to operate, subject, of course, to such qualifications in its application as the war may make necessary."

Then I come to the question of private finance, about which I have said the following:

"In belligerent countries, and particularly in Great Britain and France, the war cannot fail to have the most serious effect on the extent to which private resources will be available for assisting the refugee problem. So long as the war lasts, there is no hope of a general appeal such as that made by Lord Baldwin being launched in those countries. The general feeling is one of determination to prosecute the war to a successful issue, and to devote private resources to this end. The fountain of charity will flow more freely, but the stream will be directed towards objects which are inseparably connected with the war, such as Red Cross activities, and there will be little, if any, disposition to divert assistance to other channels. Such help as is given will be of an individual character and small in amount. Moreover, the large changes which the war has already created in the circumstances of individuals, and the still greater uncertainty which it creates concerning the future, are very effective influences at the present time. These

considerations must inevitably bring practically to an end
new contributions from the general public.

On the other hand, it is to be hoped that existing commitments will generally be honored, and that private individuals or groups of individuals who have given guarantees
for the maintenance of refugees, whether adults or children,
will continue to honor them, although cases will arise in
which the guarantor is unable to do so owing to the change
in his material circumstances."

I may say that so far in England there have been comparatively few cases in which guarantors have resiled from
the guarantees they have given. That has been one very
satisfactory feature of the past two months. It is particularly true of children, and of course most of the
children who are now in England, and there are from 9 to 10
thousand of them, are being maintained by private guarantors.
So far the war has not seriously affected that side of the
problem.

But apart from that, there doesn't seem much hope, in
fact there is practically no hope, that the general public
will be either willing or able to subscribe as it has done
in the past, towards refugee relief.

As far as one can see at present, similar considerations will affect the extent to which Jewish sources in
Great Britain are willing or able to continue the very
generous assistance they have given hitherto. It seems

127

probable that British Jewry, for instance, will regard it as their first duty to assist with their resources towards the prosecution of the war, and that they will take the view that they are not justified in accepting new commitments unless these can be shown to be directly relevant to the furtherance of the war. It seems probable that the efforts of Jewish communities in Great Britain and France will at best be restricted to the maintenance and support of the refugees at present in those countries, and to the provision within available resources of the costs of emigration for a limited number of individuals.

128

Little information has been received of the effect of the war on private contributions in neutral European countries of temporary refuge. The countries mainly affected are Holland, Belgium and Switzerland. It is to be apprehended that the private organizations of those countries will find it more difficult to raise the funds necessary for maintenance and support, and that they will have to ask for greater help from external bodies such as the Joint Distribution Committee, and, at the same time, to seek relief through emigration to countries of permanent settlement. It may be hoped that, in addition to the United States of America, the neutral countries, and in particular the Scandinavian countries, will maintain the splendid humanitarian traditions of the past.

Mr. McDonald: If you wish, I might supplement briefly what Sir Herbert has said.

First, I should like - I shouldn't like, but I must - to confirm his rather pessimistic estimate of the effect of the war on private resources for emigration purposes from the European countries. The British-Jewish groups have already indicated to the Jewish groups in this country that they will not be able to continue to contribute to overseas activities. Similarly, I am almost certain that in France and in the other countries contiguous to Germany, the Jewish organizations will be forced to take the same line, that is, as Sir Herbert has said, that their contributions can not go beyond the needs within their own countries and probably may prove to be inadequate for those limited purposes.

Hence, we reach the conclusion that private funds will be limited, if not exclusively, then nearly so, to those which can be raised in this country.

One other preliminary consideration. It is that the private funds from this country are already being more heavily drained, as Sir Herbert has said, by special conditions arising from the war. Hence the war normally will tend to reduce the private funds in this country available for emigration purposes.

There is just one possibility that that may ultimately change the conditions. If there should be organized in this country, and it is not yet in prospect and may never come to

129

be a reality, a great interdenominational war appeal such as we had during the World War when the Red Cross, the Knights of Columbus, the Catholics, and many others, were united in a great effort to raise many millions of dollars for relief in the war-stricken countries, irrespective of race and religion. In that event some relief might be given to the strain upon the Jewish organizations. But that is only a possibility and it may never become a reality.

With those preliminaries in mind, I think one could summarize the prospect of private financing in words something like these.

130

The only financing by private organizations in sight at the present time is that which will cover the cost of trial settlements in the two projects reported on yesterday, the Dominican Republic and the Philippines. It is hoped, however, that once the flow of settlers is started, certain resources of the refugees themselves, in funds supplied by relatives, will continue the flow of settlers beyond the trial numbers at the start; but thereafter we shall probably soon reach a point of cost beyond the capacity of private funds to meet.

And I should be derelict in my duty if I did not report to the Committee the strong feeling of the private organizations in this country that they can not, no matter what the necessity or the pressure, continue to bear indefinitely the full burden of emigration and settlement

They just can not.

Sir Herbert has indicated that the private organizations have already provided, he estimates, approximately 15 million pounds, which is approximately $75,000,000. That is really a very large amount of money to come from private organizations. If they were here speaking for themselves, they would, I think simply underline, perhaps more emphatically, the words which I have used.

His Excellency Count de Saint-Quentin: What period does this cover?

Mr. McDonald: From the beginning of the Hitler regime.

His Excellency Count de Saint-Quentin: From private organizations in this country?

Mr. McDonald: No, generally, including France, Great Britain, Holland, and so on.

Lord Winterton: Well, I don't know that we can carry the matter any further. We have heard two very interesting statements from the Director and from Mr. McDonald.

His Excellency Count de Saint-Quentin: On similar occasions yesterday and today, Sir Herbert Emerson told us of what the situation was in Great Britain, and, he added, presumably in France. I want to say, in every instance, "presumably" should be read "certainly". I take the opportunity of this remark to pay tribute to Sir Herbert for the very objective and illuminating manner in which he explained those difficult problems. I am also pleased to

131

express my high appreciation of the statements that Mr. McDonald made.

Lord Winterton: I should like to associate myself with what you have just said, Ambassador, and I think we might pay a tribute to the wonderful work on the part of the private organizations in all the countries in this great humane work.

Mr. Taylor: I am sure our Government would like to be associated with that thought, Mr. Chairman.

(Sir Herbert Emerson then presented memoranda pertaining to Items 2, 3, 4 and 5 of the agenda:)

132

ITEM 2 OF THE AGENDA

THE PRESENT STATUS OF PLANS FOR SETTLEMENT

Memorandum by the Director

At the session of the Intergovernmental Committee
held in July 1939, the Director made a statement regarding
the prospects of settlement in various countries. This
statement is reproduced below, with such modifications
as are necessary to bring it up to date.

British Guiana.

As regards British Guiana, the position is as follows.
In pursuance of the offer made by His Majesty's Government
in the United Kingdom in November 1938 of facilities for
the settlement of refugees in British Guiana, a Commission
assembled at Georgetown, British Guiana, on February 14
and completed its report on April 19th of this year. The
Commission was organized by President Roosevelt's Advisory
Committee on Political Refugees and included two
representatives appointed by his Majesty's government and
one by the Government of British Guiana. The Commission
expressed the view that, while the territory is not an
ideal place for refugees from Middle-European countries,
and while it could not be considered suitable for immediate
large-scale settlement, it undoubtedly possesses potential
possibilities that would fully justify the carrying out of
a trial settlement project in order to determine whether
and how these possibilities could be realized. In particular,

133

it considered that in the area available for settlement
there are soils suitable for permanent agriculture and
natural resources which make possible a correlated industrial
development, while climatic and health conditions are such
that settlement by people of Middle European origin is
feasible. At the same time, it made it clear that there
were various questions which required clarification, and
to which answers could only be given by means of a trial
settlement on the spot. They therefore recommended that a
number of receiving camps for trial settlement should be
started, involving a population of 3,000 to 5,000 carefully
selected young men and women and placed at properly chosen
locations; that these trial settlements should be adequately
equipped under competent leadership; and that they should
contain a number of people with specialized training who
would be capable of securing the necessary information and
would also assist in making the settlements self-contained.
It estimated the approximate cost of establishing and
maintaining the trial settlements for a period of two years
with a population of 5,000 people would be ₤ 600,000. His
Majesty's Government in the United Kingdom, after consideration of the Report of the Commission, has expressed
itself in complete sympathy with the scheme of refugee
settlement in British Guiana, and has stated its readiness
to place very large areas at the disposal of private
organizations for this purpose, and further, if the scheme

134

develops, to allow a large measure of authonomy in local government. It has also undertaken, when the stage of large scale settlement is reached, to provide arterial communications, on the understanding that the cost of settlement will be met from private sources.

The position as regards British Guiana is therefore, briefly, as follows: A Commission composed of highly qualified specialists has reported that the possibilities are sufficiently good to justify the carrying out of experimental settlements, and while it does not feel justified in giving any assurance as regarding the success of these, it does consider that, if they are successful, the ultimate prospect of the territory, as an area for settlement on a big scale, are very large. Before the outbreak of war, the organizations concerned had under consideration practical plans for trial settlement, and discussions were taking place with the British Colonial Office. The war has resulted in the indefinite postponement of the scheme.

135

The Dominican Republic

As regards the Dominican Republic, in pursuance of the very generous offer of the Dominican Government to admit one hundred thousand refugees, a Commission under the auspices of President Roosevelt's Advisory Committee on Political Refugees visited the Dominican Republic from March 7th to April 18th of this year. The Commission was

given active assistance by the Dominican Government and
investigated seventeen tracts of land which had been
indicated as available for settlement, a total area amounting
to about 2,700,000 acres. Of this area some 2,150,000 acres
are owned by the Government while about half a million acres
are privately owned. It appeared that, if necessary, other
areas adjacent to certain of the tracts could be made
available for settlement. The Commission has reported that
climatic conditions are favourable for colonists from Central
Europe, and that health conditions are reasonably good. It
found the soil in a number of tracts highly fertile and
capable of producing a large variety of crops, for some of
which there is a commercial demand. Valuable forest products
are readily accessible in large volume. While the Commission
did not find that the whole of the area suggested was
suitable for early colonisation, it considered that it would
be possible to settle approximately 29,000 families in certain
specified areas on a subsistence basis. At the same time
it stressed the fact that, before proceeding on a big scale
with the plans for colonization, it would be necessary to
carry out technical studies in topography, soils, drainage,
agronomy, sanitation and forestplanning. It was recommended
that the first step should be the establishment of pioneering
groups of perhaps 200 or 250 persons each in camps similar
to those of the Civilian Conservation Corps in the United
States

Subsequently the Dominican Republic, as a first step towards the realization of her desire to accept substantial number of refugees, offered to receive immediately 500 families to be divided as follows:

(a) Agricultural families with the parents between 25 and 30 years of age, adequate provision to be made for their long-term acquisition of suitable land.

(b) Professional families, the parents ranging from 25 to 40 years of age.

(c) Families adaptable to the development of various industrial and manufacturing enterprises.

(d) Individuals of miscellaneous categories suitable to the needs of the Republic.

137

(e) Children between the ages of 13 and 15, who would be wards of the Government for a period of two years, with the Government providing the resources for their maintenance, towards the end that they may be eventually intergrated into the economic and agricultural life of the country.

It is understood that President Roosevelt's Advisory Committee on Political Refugees has established a Committee to carry out negotiations with the representative in Washington of the Dominican Republic.

Although, therefore, large scale settlement must inevitably move slowly in the initial stages, it appears that a beginning of pioneer settlement can be made when a final agreement is concluded with the Dominican Republic and the necessary funds are forthcoming.

<u>Northern Rhodesia.</u>

As regards Northern Rhodesia, a Committee was formed by the Emigration (Planning) Joint Committee of the Co-ordinating Committee for Refugees, an association which has its head-quarters in London. It assembled in the Colony on March 29th and concluded its Report on June 1st. It was greatly assisted by the Government of the Colongy, who made available the services of their Director of Agriculture and the Directory of Veterinary Services. The Commission found no serious climatic or physical obstacles to settlement, but considered that settlement should be limited only be economic factors. It recommended that the individual holdings should be sufficiently large to allow for subsistence with the addition of a small cash margin sufficient to repay over a long period advances made for settlement and to leave a small surplus for other expenses. It expressed the view that not more than 400 to 500 families could be settled over a period of years without disturbance of the economic system of the Colony, and it estimated that the cost of establishing a family and of maintaining it during an initial period would be from Ł 1,000 to Ł 1,500.

It would therefore appear from the Report of the Commission that this area is not suitable for large-scale settlement, and that the cost of individual settlement would be high. Even if immigration had otherwise been feasible, the war will make the situation more difficult because of political considerations and of the distrust with which persons of German origin or nationality would be regarded.

ITEM 3 OF THE AGENDA

Memorandum by the Director

The question whether or not the Possibilities for
Individual Emigration and either Group or Mass Settlement
so far Developed are Adequate to meet the Problem.

- -

140

(1) As explained in a separate memorandum, the emigration
of refugees from Greater Germany has outstripped the
opportunities for permanent settlement, with the result that
the number in countries of temporary refuge was continuously
increasing. None the less, since 1933 approximately 250,000
had found permanent homes. At least ninety per cent of these
had been placed by infiltration, and with the exception of
Palestine, and to a lesser extent of the Argentine, there
had been little group settlement on any considerable scale.
Outside Europe, infiltration had been almost general, and
there were few countries which had not received refugees in
greater or smaller numbers. Some of these had already
reached or were approaching the point of saturation, but
even so, the flow of emigrants was not entirely stopped,
since those refugees who were well established were often
able to secure for their near relatives. The main places
of settlement were the United States of America, Palestine,
Australia and the countries of South America. The total
rate of infiltration was not constant. For instance, several
of the states of South America from time to time imposed

restrictions on immigration either by amendment of the law or by tightening up its administration. One reason for this was the fact that immigrants included a certain number of unsuitable persons, while, owing to the rush of refugees from Germany, the private organizations were not always able to organize or to finance emigration as thoroughly as was desirable. There were some opportunities for individual settlement which it had not been possible to utilize owing to difficulties of finance. The Government of Brazil, for instance, had made a very generous offer to receive 3,000 confessional Jews and 3,000 Catholics of semitic origin; but up to the commencement of the war it had not been possible to take advantage of this offer.

141

The general position previous to the war was one of uncertainty. Given orderly emigration from Germany, and the continuance of the generous policy shown by many countries, the problem was capable of solution within a reasonable period. There had, however, been no real mitigation of the disorderly and brutal methods pursued by Germany, and there was a very definite threat of their extension to Bohemia, Moravia and Slovakia. There was also no guarantee that various countries could continue to absorb refugees at the same rate. There was also the danger of outbursts of antisemitic feeling which would check, if not stop immigration It was therefore necessary to explore the possibilities of settlement on a large scale in order, first to relieve the

growing pressure on countries of temporary asylum, and
secondly, to ensure against contraction of the openings
for individual settlement.

(2) The war has very materially changed the position.
The problem of direct emigration from Germany is likely
to be in abeyance. The immediate problem is one of re-
emigration from countries of temporary refuge. It may be
that, so far as Great Britain and France are concerned, the
problem of re-emigration may prove not to be so urgent as
before the war, and that the Governments of those countries
may be able to place in useful employment many of their
temporary visitors. It may, however, be assumed that the
neutral countries of Europe will wish to be relieved as
early as possible of a serious embarrassment, that they
will be unable to allow refugees in any large number to
seek employment, and that in the interests of the Governments
concerned and of the refugees themselves, it will be
desirable that permanent places of settlement should be
found as rapidly as possible.

While the war has reduced the size of the problem
coming within the present scope of the Committee's activities
it seems inevitable that it will also reduce the number of
openings for emigration previously available. The belligerent
countries will now have to give first and foremost
consideration to political factors, and to determine question
of immigration into their territories with primary reference

to the effect it may have on the general situation. In so far as emigration may still be possible, considerations of safety may be expected to prevail, and one may anticipate that the selection of immigrants of German origin or nationality will have to be carried out far more rigorously than before the war. It may not be possible for them to determine the general lines of policy at once, and in any case they would be liable to modification.

(3) So far as neutral countries of permanent settlement are concerned, it may be hoped that circumstances will not arise which will make it necessary to restrict the generous policy they have hiterto pursued, and that they may be able even to extend the openings previously available. Should this prove to be the case, a large measure of success can be achieved in finding at least a war-time solution of the problem of refugees from Greater Germany, as it has been modified by a state of war.

143

ITEM 4 OF THE AGENDA

Memorandum by the Director

POSSIBILITIES OF LARGE-SCALE SETTLEMENT IN AREAS ALREADY
CONSIDERED ON IN OTHER AREAS.

In the Memorandum relating to the second item on the
agenda prospects have been stated of large-scale settlement
in areas which have already been investigated. With regard
to other possibilities for large-scale settlement, several
factors have to be considered before a country can be regarded both as suitable and available. Political considerations have an important bearing on the question. There are
some countries which are prima facie suitable for settlement
on a considerable scale, but are either unwilling to receive
refugees, or are willing to receive them in limited numbers
or by infiltration. Unless there is a change of policy on
the part of the Governments concerned, the possibilities must
be regarded as too vague for practical purposes. There are
other countries which must be clearly ruled out of account
for climatic reasons. There are again others in regard to
which there has been no final statement of policy, and which
might be willing to receive refugees in considerable numbers
if it were possible to place before them well considered
schemes which would be assured of adequate finance. For
the present purposes it will probably be sufficient to
confine attention to possibilities which previous to the
war were sufficiently tangible to merit further investigation.

144

(a) A preliminary enquiry has been carried out into the possibilities of permanent settlement in an island of the <u>Philippines</u>. It is understood that further enquiry will be necessary before definite plans can be formulated.

(b) There has been reason to suppose that the Government of <u>Ecuador</u> would be favourably disposed towards the settlement of refugees if a satisfactory scheme were placed before them. An accredited representative visited London a few months ago, when he discussed with the High Commissioner of the League of Nations and private organisations various proposals for settlement. Later, on his return to Ecuador, he asked the High Commissioner to arrange for a representative of the private organisations to confer with the Settlement Committee that was to be set up. The Ministry for the Colonies and the Central Bank of Ecuador were to have representations on this Committee. The scheme was said to contemplate the settlement of 10,000 families. The matter was referred through the British Emigration Planning Committee to the President's Advisory Committee for Political Refugees, and it is not known what progress has been made. While it is open to doubt whether the proposals so far made on behalf of the Ecuador Government are suitable, and in particular, whether the lands proposed for settlement are, from the point of view of climate, accessibility and communications, capable of colonisation by Europeans, there is reason to believe

145

that direct negotiations with the Government of Ecuador
might be successful in attaining a practical scheme, if the
finance of such a scheme were assured.

(c)   From time to time suggestions have been made for
colonisation in various states of South America, some of
which have taken a large number of refugees by infiltration,
e.g. Paraguay, Bolivia and Chile. It has not been possible
for financial reasons to put before the Governments of these
states self-contained schemes which would admit of the
settlement of considerable numbers.

(d)   With the approval of the French Government, an
investigation was being made of the possibilities of settlement in New Caledonia, but this had not proceeded sufficiently
far for an opinion to be formed regarding the prospects.

The above was the position at the end of August. It is
inevitable that the war should raise new considerations. Most
Governments will wish to review their previous policy regarding entry into their own territories. Again, while the emigration of persons of German origin or nationality into some
countries might be desirable in normal times, it may raise
political issues during a state of war. It is not possible
at present to make any estimate of value of the prospects of
large-scale settlement in any country.

146

———————

ITEM 5 OF THE AGENDA.

Memorandum by the Director

The Problem of Financing Emigration and Settlement, includ-

ing the Possibilities of Governmental

Participation.

I.   The Position previous to the War.

1.   The methods of financing the refugee problem
previous to the war were described by me in a memorandum
written about the middle of July 1939, which I handed over
to Mr. Wohlthat.   This is reproduced below, with a few
verbal amendments.

147

A.

Governmental
Assistance.

The emigration of refugees from Czecho-Slovakia has
been largely financed from the gift of ₤4,000,000 made
by the British Government.   The Belgian Government has
undertaken the maintenance of 3,000 of the refugees who
had been given temporary asylum in that country.   The
Dutch Government has undertaken the construction of a
central training camp at large cost for the training and
accomodation of a large number of refugees who have
similarly received temporary asylum.   For the rest,
governmental assistance has been practically confined
to the expansion of the necessary administrative services

to deal with immigration into their countries, and the grant of facilities for training camps and for housing accomodation on Government property or in Government buildings. Where emigration has been to countries of permanent refuge, e.g. British colonies, some expansion has been necessary of administrative services.

The British Government has accepted the contingent and very large liability for the provision of arterial communications in British Guiana when immigration there reaches the state of large-scale settlement.

B.

148

Liabilities for
which private bodies
are responsible.

Apart from the above, and the resources which refugees have themselves been able to provide, the finance of the movement has depended on charitable funds from private sources. These have had to finance, wholly or in part, expenditure on the following objects:

(1) Relief in the country of origin.

(2) Relief and maintenance in the countries of temporary refuge.

(3) The cost of training.

(4) Relief and maintenance in countries of permanent refuge for those who cannot at once earn their own livelihood.

(5) Expenses of transport, visas, etc. to countries
of refuge.

(6) Expenses connected with the permanent settlement of refugees, whether by individual or group
settlement.

(7) Overhead expenses.

There are hundreds of organizations working in various
countries - Jewish, non-Jewish, and non-sectarian. Some
are concerned only with the raising and allocation of
funds; others are concerned purely with executive work
and get the necessary funds from the financing organizations; others again combine the two functions. In England,
for example, there is, apart from the large central organizations, a large number of local committees which
raise the whole or part of their funds by local appeals.
The same is the case in other countries.

There is another method of charitable contribution
which, while it cannot be assessed accurately in cash,
represents a very large sum, namely, the system of private
hospitality, by which a family, a group or families, or
a small committee acepts financial responsibility for the
support and maintenance of individual refugees, and also
in some cases the liability for the expenses of emigration.
Many gifts have also been made in kind.

There are very few organizations at present with

149

independent finance which are concerned solely or even mainly with emigration and settlement.

Among these may be mentioned the following:

(1) The Jewish Colonisation Association (J.C.A.)

This administers a trust fund created some years ago for the purpose of the colonisation of Jews. Under the terms of the Trust the capital cannot be expended. The income is available for the colonisation of Jews in general, and during recent years a large part of it has been used for the colonisation of migrants from German territory, especially in South America. It has spent approximately Ł900,000 in connection with German refugees, of which about Ł800,000 has been spent on emigration and settlement.

150

(2) The Jewish Agency for Palestine.

The Jewish Agency has a branch known as the Bureau for the Settlement of German Jews in Palestine. Up to the end of 1938 the Bureau had spent approximately Ł1,000,000 directly for this purpose. Large sums have been spent indirectly for the same purpose by the Jewish Agency.

(3) The Refugee Economic Corporation of America.

This was formed in 1934, and up to the middle of 1938 about Ł50,000 of the authorised capital had been subscribed. The Corporation has fianced the requirements of a number of individual settlers.

(4) The Plough Settlement of Kenya.

The subscribed capital of Ł10,000, the authorised capital Ł25,000. The Corporation has financed the settle-ment of a certain number of refugees in Kenya.

Among the organizations which are concerned with maintenance and relief as well as with emigration and settlement, the following may be mentioned:

(1) The American Jewish Joint Distribution Committee.

This Committee was formed in 1914, and throughout the war and in the year following it did relief work of enormous value in the countries of Europe. It is financed by private charity in the United States of America and Canada, where an annual appeal is made for funds. I have not the figures for total expenditure up-to-date. But up to the end of December 1937 it had received and spent approximately Ł18,000,000. Of late years a considerable part of its income has been spent on work connected with refugees from German territory. A good deal of its work is done through direct agency, but it also grants very liberal subsidies to many organisations. Since 1933 it has spent more than Ł2,000,000 in connection with German migrants. Its yearly expenditure on this work has increased from approximately Ł80,000 in 1933 to Ł540,000 in 1938. During the first five months of 1939 it has already spent nearly as much as it did during the whole of 1938, and its budget for 1939 is based on a programme of Ł1,600,000.

(2) The Council for German Jewry.

This body was established in 1936 in order to organize support by the principal Jewish communities of the world for the emigration and training of German Jews. It took over most of the activities of the Central British Fund for German Jewry, which was formed in 1933 and was a purely British association. A general appeal has been made each year since 1933, except in the year 1937, in which no appeal was made since a special appeal was made in the previous year. Associated with the appeals of the Council there has been a Women's Committee, which has issued an appeal each year for women and children refugees. The total sum raised since 1933 amounts approximately to £2,750,000. The greater part of this has been spent assisting emigration through grants to various associations.

152

(3) The leading Jewish organisation in Holland, namely the Comité voor Bijzondere Joodsche Belangen has collected approximately £400,000 since 1933, of which rather more than £50,000 has been spent on emigration, the rest being required for the maintenance of refugees inside Holland.

Other organisations which have collected substantial sums are:

The Christian Council for Refugees from
Germany and Central Europe   £80,000

The Society of Friends, Germany
Emergency Committee   £59,000

International Hebrew Christian Alliance   Ł25,000

Verband. Schweiz. Israel. Armenpflegen   Ł121,000

Schweizer. Hilfswerk fur Emigrantenkinder   Ł30,000

Of the general appeals not sponsored by any specific organisation, special mention may be made of the Baldwin Appeal, to which subscriptions have been made exceeding Ł500,000

Figures are available for a few only of the many hundreds of small organisations that have made appeals. In the aggregate the sum collected by them has been large.

It is possible to make only a rough estimate of the total receipts of the charitable organisations. Their collections may be put at a minimum of Ł10,000,000 in cash. Taking into account the cost of hospitality, gifts in kind etc., the total contribution is not less than Ł15,000,000, and may be considerably higher.

153

By far the greater part of this amount has been subscribed by the Jewish community through successive appeals made by a number of organisations.

2. In addition to the above organisations, mention must be made of the Co-ordinating Foundation, a Trust Company registered in London with a capital of Ł200,000. The aims and objects of the Foundation have been stated in a very wide and general form. It was anticipated that the main function of the Foundation would be to act as

a link between the private organisations and the Internal Trust when established in Germany and that, in particular, it should act as the purchasing agency mentioned in the Confidential Memorandum communicated to Mr. Rublee. It was not intended that the Foundation should directly finance emigration, but its aims include the conduct of negotiations with Governments and private bodies for the purpose of furthering the permanent settlement of refugees. Proposals had in fact been made to Mr. van Zeeland, President of the Foundation, and its chief executive officer, that it should take up discussions with various Governments regarding the admission of refugees. The war prevented effect being given to these proposals, which are at present in abeyance.

154

3. Previous to the war the financial position was, briefly, as follows: With slight exceptions the whole burden of financing the movement was being borne by the private organisations. The non-Jewish organisations were reaching the end of their resources and were in fact unable to provide for the contingent liabilities which they had accepted regarding the emigration of refugees in temporary countries or refuge. The position of the Jewish bodies was increasingly difficult. Although private contributions had tended to increase, the growth of expenditure was greater than the growth of resources. This was due to the ever increasing number of refugees in countries of temporary refuge inside

and outside Europe who were dependent for their maintenance
and support on private charity. As a result the organizations were finding it increasingly difficult to finance
existing commitments, and were unable to provide the funds
on a sufficient scale necessary to finance emigration.
Their policy was inevitably a hand-to-mouth one, and they were
unable to take a long view of the situation or to present to
countries of permanent settlement fully considered schemes,
backed by adequate finance over a term of years, which might
offer an inducement to them to pursue a more liberal policy.
At the same time, the Governments of those countries which
had given temporary asylum to large numbers of refugees found
themselves in a position of growing embarrassment. There
was a lag between admission of refugees and their emigration
and, as the number of alien Jews increased, the dangers grew
of antisemitic feeling.

155

    4. It was in these circumstances that, at the meeting
of the Intergovernmental Committee held in London in July
1939, the Right Honourable the Earl Winterton M.P., Chairman
of the Committee, made the following statement as Representative on the Committee of His Majesty's Government in the United
Kingdom:

"In the very interesting and comprehensive report
which he has made to the Committee, the Director has drawn
attention to two most important and disquieting factors in

the existing refugee situation. The first is the very large number of refugees who are now in the countries of refuge and who cannot possibly remain in them indefinitely I have today circulated to the Committee a memorandum in which it is estimated that there are now 40,000 refugees in this country, of whom at least half, if not more, must eventually be re-emigrated. The Committee knows that in the other countries of immediate refuge, the Netherlands, Belgium, France, Switzerland, Denmark, thanks to the very generous policy of the various Governments, there are many thousands of refugees who have been admitted to those countries, but who cannot settle permanently in Europe. Sir Herbert Emerson estimated that there are 150,000 refugees from Greater Germany in other European countries, and that approximately 60,000 of these are wholly or partly dependent on the charity of the private associations.

156

2. "This leads me to the second disquieting factor in the situation, namely that of finance. The vast number of refugees who must be supported in the countries of refuge are proving a very heavy burden to the private organisations which have hitherto borne the cost of their maintenance. So heavy is the burden that the private organisations are finding it exceedingly difficult to make any large payments for the permanent settlement of refugees either by infiltration or group settlement. The result is a vicious

circle. No long term policy of financing emigration
overseas is possible because the burden of maintenance in
countries of refuge is crippling the resources of the private organizations, while the cost of maintenance cannot
be reduced so long as the rate of emigration overseas is
inferior to the rate of immigration into countries of refuge
from Germany.

3. "The result is that we are now faced with the possibility of a serious interruption in the procedure regarding
refugees which has been adopted by the Governments of the
countries of refuge. The voluntary organisations in those
countries have accepted responsibility for many thousands
of refugees in the expectation that they would be able to
emigrate within a fairly short time. This expectation has
not been fulfilled to anything like the extent anticipated,
and the voluntary organisations are left with financial
commitments which are so heavy that it is difficult to see
how they can be met. Thus they are unable to undertake any
further commitments for the constructive expenditure which
is essential if the rate of emigration overseas is to be
maintained or increased.

4. "His Majesty's Government in the United Kingdom have
given very careful consideration to the serious situation
which has come about. It is clearly necessary that large
sums should be raised for the emigration of refugees but in

157

existing circumstances it is impossible for the private organisations to find these sums in the measure requisite for
a satisfactory solution of the problem. His Majesty's
Government in the United Kingdom have therefore reached the
conclusion that unless the work of the Committee is to be
seriously obstructed and the countries of refuge are to be
left with large numbers of refugees who cannot be absorbed,
it will be necessary to depart from the principle agreed
unanimously at Evian, that no participating Government would
give direct financial assistance to refugees.

5. "His Majesty's Government are, for their part
examining the manner and extent to which private subscription
to an international fund to assist in defraying the expenses
of overseas emigration of refugees might be encouraged by
Government participation, possibly on a basis proportionate
to the amount of private subscription, and I would earnestly
invite my colleagues to lay these considerations before their
Governments and to communicate their views to me without delay. If other Governments are prepared to agree to this
change of principle, and to cooperate in such participation,
His Majesty's Government in the United Kingdom will take the
initiative in proposing a scheme for the purpose."

2. The effects of the War on the Finance of Emigration
    and Settlement.

158

Governmental
Assistance.

It is understood that in view of the war His Majesty's
Government in the United Kingdom find it impossible to
contemplate any new financial commitments which are not
directly related to its prosecution, and that therefore
they cannot usefully proceed at present with the formulation of the scheme for financial assistance mentioned in
the statement of the Right Honourable the Earl Winterton,
M.P., reproduced above. On the other hand, so far as refugees in England are concerned, it is hoped that the
liberal policy adopted by the British Government will result in many of them becoming self-supporting, and will
thus afford relief to the private organisations. In so far
as it may be necessary to intern a certain number, they
would be a charge on the state, and the same is presumably
true of those interned in France. It is understood that
the Trust Fund which has been constituted by His Majesty's
Government in the United Kingdom to assist refugees from
Czecho-Slovakia, until such time as the balance of the
British loan becomes available, will continue to operate,
subject of course to such modifications in its application
as the war may make necessary.

Private
Finance.

In belligerent countries, and particularly in Great

159

Britain and France, the war cannot fail to have the most
serious effect on the extent to which private resources
will be available for assisting the refugee problem. So
long as the war lasts there is no hope of a general appeal
such as that made by Lord Baldwin being launched in those
countries. The general feeling is one of determination to
prosecute the war to a successful issue, and to devote private resources to this end. The fountain of charity will
flow more freely, but the stream will be directed towards
objects which are inseparably connected with the war, such
as Red Cross activities, and there will be little if any
disposition to divert assistance to other channels. Such
help as is given will be of an individual character and
small in amount. Moreover, the large changes which the
war has already created in the circumstances of individuals,
and the still greater uncertainty which it creates concerning the future are very effective influences at the present
time. These considerations must inevitably bring practically
to an end new contributions from the general public. On the
other hand, it is to be hoped that existing commitments will
generally be honoured, and that private individuals or groups
of individuals who have given guarantees for the maintenance
of refugees, whether adults or children, will continue to
honour them, although cases will arise in which the guarantor
is unable to do so owing to the change in his material

160

circumstances.

Similar considerations will affect the extent to which Jewish sources are willing or able to continue the very generous assistance they have given hitherto. It seems probable that British Jewry, for instance, will regard it as their first duty to assist with their resources towards the prosecution of the war, and that they will take the view that they are not justified in accepting new commitments unless these can be shown to be directly relevant to the furtherance of the war. It seems probable that the efforts of the Jewish communities in Great Britain and France will at best be restricted to the maintenance and support of the refugees at present in those countries, and to the provision within available resources of the costs of emigration for a limited number of individuals.

Little information has been received of the effect of the war on the private contributions in neutral European countries of temporary refuge. The countries mainly affected are Holland, Belgium and Switzerland. It is to be apprehended that the private organisations of those countries will find it more difficult to raise the funds necessary for maintenance and support, and that they will have to ask for greater help from external bodies such as the Joint Distribution Committee and, at the same time, to seek relief through emigration to countries of permanent

settlement. It may be hoped that, in addition to the United
States of America, the neutral countries, and in particular
the Scandinavian countries, will maintain the splendid
humanitarian traditions of the past. (memorandum ends)

Lord Winterton: Well, gentlemen, there remains the
last item on the agenda, and I would wish to submit to my
colleagues a suggestion on that point. The last item of
the agenda, taken in conjunction with the President's em-
phatic reference in his speech yesterday, and the subject
matter of it, raises questions of great importance and magnitude as I said yesterday. It is so important that I would
like to requote to my colleagues what the President has said
in connection with this Item 6:

"I have suggested that the current task is small in
comparison with the future task. The war will come to an
end some day; and those of us who are realists know that
in its wake the world will face a refugee problem of different character and of infinitely greater magnitude.

"Nearly every great war leaves behind it vast numbers
of human beings whose roots have been literally torn up.
Inevitably there are great numbers of individuals who
have lost all family ties -- individuals who find no home
to return to, no occupation to resume -- individuals who
for many different reasons must seek to rebuild their

162

lives under new environments.

"Every war leaves behind it tens of thousands of families who for very many different reasons are compelled to start life anew in other lands.

"Economic considerations may affect thousands of families and individuals.

"All we can do is to estimate on the reasonable doctrine of chance, that when this ghastly war ends there may be not one million but ten million or twenty million men, women and childred belonging to many races and many religions, living in many countries and possibly on several continents, who will enter into the wide picture -- the problem of the human refugee.

163

"I ask, therefore, that as the second great task that lies before this Committee, it start at this time a serious and probably a fairly expansive effort to survey and study definitely and scientifically this geographical and economic problem of resettling several million people in new areas of the earth's surface."

My Government would wish to give most complete and sympathetic consideration to any proposals made by the United States Government in this connection. But they would have to be considered, if justice is to be done, in a concrete form. I therefore invite the American delegation, if they would be good enough to do so, to prepare a draft of these proposals. It ought then, I submit, to be considered by our expert advisers in consultation with our Acting Secretary, Mr. Morris, because the question of the constitution of the Committee must inevitably arise, and they will have to consider what change, if any, would be necessary to give effect to any proposals made. Then we could meet in conference next week to hear their report. Even so, we might very likely have to consult our Governments before we can make a recommendation to the whole Committee.

In suggesting this course, I am most anxious to avoid giving the impression of wanting to delay a decision. On the contrary, I feel, both as Chairman and as the United Kingdom representative, that in courtesy alike to the President and to our hosts, the United States Government, we ought to give immediate and complete consideration to any proposal made so that the decision may be reached at the earliest possible time; but I think the procedure suggested will most effectively achieve this result.

Mr. Taylor: Mr. Chairman, we are very sympathetic with the suggestion which you have made that the discussion of this matter, Item 6, be postponed until the meeting of next week, and that in the interim a technical committee be set up and have its report ready for next Wednesday or Thursday, whichever day you appoint for the meeting. I think that a technical committee made up of representatives of the Government that are participants in this conference, will be able to clear away a great many uncertainties and produce something that will be useful and constructive for our consideration at that time. It seems to me that to engage in a discussion of it in advance of that would lead us down perhaps many wrong paths that we could very easily avoid by the other procedure.

The Honorable Dr. Loudon: May I ask one thing more? I have been instructed by my Government that, under the present circumstances, they do not consider it advisable to extend the scope of the Committee because this might lead to consequences which, owing to the war, cannot be foreseen. This instruction, of course, was received before I listened to the speech of the President of the United States. Now, if we are going to discuss the report of a technical committee next week, I would very much appreciate it if it could be arranged to have the report circulated one or two days before the meeting will take place in order that I may, if necessary, ask my Government for instructions.

Mr. Taylor: Could not the Technical Committee meet on Friday of this week?

Lord Winterton: Certainly, Mr. Taylor.

Mr. Taylor: That would allow adequate time.

Lord Winterton: I should also like to consult my

165

Government similarly.

(The delegates present nominated their representatives to sit on the Technical Committee).

(After a discussion of a communiqué to be issued to the press by the Intergovernmental Committee, the meeting, at 1:15 o'clock p.m., was adjourned until 3:00 o'clock p.m., Thursday, October 26, 1939).

- - - - - -

The text of the communiqué is as follows:

166

Upon the invitation of President Roosevelt the officers of the Intergovernmental Committee met at the White House on October 17, 1939. The Secretary of State opened the second meeting at the Department of State on the afternoon of October 17 and a third meeting was held on the morning of October 18 when the Committee adjourned until Thursday, October 26, 1939 Those who attended the meeting included Lord Winterton, Chairman and Paymaster General in the British Government; Sir Herbert Emerson, Director; the Honorable Myron C. Taylor, Vice Chairman representing the United States of America; His Excellency Senor Don Felipe Espil, the Argentine Ambassador; His Excellency Count de Saint Quentin, the French Ambassador; His Excellency Mr. Carlos Martins, the Brazilian Ambassador; Dr. A. Loudon, the Netherlands Minister; and Mr. James G. McDonald, Chairman of the President's Advisory Committee on Political Refugees.

The meeting, at the second session, heard a report on the current refugee situation by the Director and discussed the various ways in which the refugee problem might be met. Particular attention was given to the new aspects of the situation due to the outbreak of war.

At the third session, the officers discussed what President Roosevelt had described in his opening statement as the "short-range problem", including the problem of emigrating those individuals and families who are at this moment in countries of temporary refuge and who, for the sake of the world and themselves, should be placed in permanent domiciles as rapidly as possible.

167

The meeting was of the opinion that this problem could still best be solved partly by infiltration, that is individual immigration, and partly by an initiation of settlement projects. The meeting took note, with particular satisfaction, of the fact that the Dominican Government, with great foresight and generosity, had responded to the appeal of the Intergovernmental Committee for opportunities of settlement. The meeting also heard with satisfaction that the Government of the Commonwealth of the Philippines had responded in a similar manner. Mr. McDonald reported that engineering and economic studies had recently been completed and that practical steps, including financing, in the initiation of settlement were being taken.

The meeting was informed that similar studies in other areas would be undertaken promptly.

The Committee also took note of the fact that the Coordinating Foundation, whose Executive President, Mr. Paul van Zeeland, will be present at the meeting next week, is mandated to work with individuals and organizations to investigate the suitability of places of settlement and future resettlement plans.

A tribute was paid by the meeting to the unstinted generosity over a period of years of the private organizations.

* * *

168

CONFERENCE of OFFICERS

of the

INTER-GOVERNMENTAL COMMITTEE ON POLITICAL REFUGEES

State Department,
Washington, D. C.
October 26, 1939 - 3 p.m.

- - - - - -

PRESENT

(Same as noted for the October 18, 1939,
meeting, except:

Dr. Carl Bruggmann, Minister of Switzerland - Not Present

Hon. Paul van Zeeland, President, Coordinating
Foundation - Present.

169

- - - - - -

Lord Winterton: Gentlemen, the sitting of the Conference is resumed. The first item on our agenda of today is to have the letter from the Dominican Government to the Dominican Corporation read.

Mr. Pell: Mr. Warren has the text.

Lord Winterton: I suggest it be placed in the record. Mr. Warren has copies of the letter for distribution.

Mr. Warren: I might summarize it for you very briefly. It reviews the history of the negotiations, starting with the original creation of the Inter-Governmental Committee, and then outlines the various conditions which the Dominican Government has accepted in anticipation of the organization of a corporation which will undertake the settlement of refugees. The conditions are very generous and very broadly stated, and in effect form the basis of what will later become a specific contract between the corporation to be formed and the Dominican Government.

The proposal is to undertake a trial settlement of 500 families in the first instance. Briefly, those immigrants recommended by the corporation will be exempt from the existing $500 head tax; their goods, chattels, tools and equipment will be admitted free; they will be treated as citizens and will be enabled to acquire citizenship within two years. The funds for the initial settlement have already been made available.

Lord Winterton: Gentlemen, Your Excellencies, it gives me great pleasure to learn of the progress that has been made in this scheme. I think we all hope it will prove to be a great success. I take it we all agree that this letter should be placed on the record.

(The letter referred to is as follows:)

Office of the Dominican Legation

October 25, 1939.

Mr. George L. Warren, Secretary

President's Advisory Committee on Political Refugees,
122 East 22nd Street,
New York City.

Dear Mr. Warren:

It gives me great pleasure to hand you herewith a duplicate of the letter which I have today delivered to Mr. James N. Rosenberg at the luncheon at which you, he and I have participated.

171

I take this occasion to express the deep appreciation of my government for your splendid cooperative efforts in the many conferences which we have had, and for the valuable cooperation which we have had from the President's Advisory Committee on Political Refugees, particularly of Mr. McDonald, its Chairman and of yourself, its Executive Secretary. It is needless for me to say that in the practical work of the plans which we have now agreed upon, my government and I personally are counting on the active cooperation of the President's Advisory Committee and especially on your continued and effective personal interest in this important undertaking.

Faithfully yours,

(Signed) A. PASTORIZA

October 19, 1939.

Mr. James N. Rosenberg
New York City.

Dear Mr. Rosenberg:

When the President of the United States initiated the Evian Conference a year and half ago for the noble, humanitarian purpose of aiding the resettlement of refugees, the Dominican Republic informed Mr. Myron C. Taylor of its willingness to receive and give an opportunity for livelihood and permanent homes to 100,000 refugees; such refugees to come to our country over the course of such number of years as may be necessary to enable them to establish themselves soundly and permanently as useful and self-supporting citizens of the Dominican Republic. Practical progress along these lines has only recently become possible, following the creation of the Inter-Governmental Committee, and the steps which have been taken by the nations of the world which have participated in that movement. Following our announcement to Mr. Taylor, surveys as to economic, agricultural and other opportunities in the Dominican Republic have been made at the instance of the President's Advisory Committee on Political

Refugees and upon the completion of the surveys and the favorable reports which were made as to settlement possibilities in our country, we have entered into conversations with your colleagues and yourself which have led to a definite proposal from you and them making possible the beginning of the work of settlement as soon as all preliminary arrangements can be completed.

On Tuesday last, October 17th, President Roosevelt, in welcoming Lord Winterton, Chairman of the Inter-governmental Committee, and his colleagues, stated that "active steps have been taken to begin actual settlement made possible by the generous attitude of the Dominican Government". As you know, this statement has reference to the matters which have for some time been under discussion.

173

It need hardly be said that our government is deeply appreciative of President Roosevelt's statement. We wish, however, to make it clear that the government of the Dominican Republic is not actuated only by humanitarian impulses, but by a realization that just as the United States has been built into a great nation through emigration of hardy and useful settlers and pioneers, so we in our country also recognize the need and desirability of having such pioneer refugees settle and take part in the constructive progress of our country, which has been rapid and sound during the last decade. In our various conversations with Mr. George L.

Warren, Executive Secretary of President Roosevelt's Advisory Committee on Political Refugees, yourself and your colleagues, we have all agreed that it is essential that such a settlement program should begin on a moderate scale and that it requires careful selection of the right kind of human material. Through the action of your colleagues and yourself, sufficient funds have now been allocated to make possible a beginning of this important project at an early date. Hence, it is appropriate that you should now have the following statement of the position of the Dominican Government which I have the honor to represent.

174

1.- Following the preliminary surveys made by the experts sent to my country by the President's Advisory Committee, my government invites further visits in order that fully detailed plans may be worked out with the utmost promptness.

2.- With the aid of the President's Advisory Committee and in cooperation with your colleagues and yourself, we propose that steps shall be taken overseas for the selection of a first unit of approximately five hundred refugee families, Jewish and non-Jewish. These refugee families are to be selected for their fitness in this pioneering work upon the soil which they will principally engage in, and also for their fitness in industry and production as well as in the necessary professional technical and skilled supplementation required for a balanced economy. In the discussions which

we have all had, there has been unanimity as to the wisdom of
making a modest beginning with about five hundred families so
as to avoid the pitfalls and dangers of initiating too large
an undertaking at the outset.

3.- Through appropriate legislation, I am satisfied that
my government will take such steps as to give adequate assur-
ances that such settlers shall enjoy full civic, economic
and religious rights, the same as are accorded to all citizens of my country; that they shall have the right after a
reasonably brief period, say of two years, to acquire their
naturalization in accordance with our laws. I beg to assure
you that our government, which is keenly desirous of making
this undertaking a milestone in the difficult refugee problems which confront the world, will take all appropriate
steps to see to it that there shall be no discrimination
against such settlers but that they shall be given an honorable, just and equal opportunity so that they may pursue their
occupations and life free of molestation and persecution,
and that our government will take appropriate steps to carry
out such purposes. In conformity with these general statements, our government will be prepared to take steps so that
settlers may be permitted to import, duty free, not for sale,
but for their use on the soil, such tools, equipment, materi-
als, etc. as may be needed to establish them as economically
self-supporting.

4.- As a result of the discussions with you, and according to information received from you and your colleagues, it is contemplated that at an early date a corporation will be formed by your colleagues and yourself which shall at the outset receive a sufficient amount of paid-in capital as agreed upon, to initiate the undertaking along the lines above described. Such corporation will be permitted to maintain an office, and its representative, experts and others will be accorded full rights to fully conduct this enterprise within my country. Such corporation, as all other humanitarian enterprises in my country as well as the enterprises for agricultural colonization under the control of the Department of Agriculture, will be exempted from any taxes. We shall be glad, provided the State Department of your country agrees, to give its official representatives such diplomatic or quasi-diplomatic privileges as may seem advisable. It is to be understood that the corporation shall pay or provide all the expenses for the transportation of the proposed settlers, their landing and their care on arrival in my country. We recognize that temporary housing may have to be provided for such settlers. To that end, my government will allocate an adequate piece of land for the free use of the settlers for an initial, reasonable period of time until they shall find their permanent homes. We shall facilitate in every way the efforts of the corporation

176

to be formed, in the selection and erection of such suitable
housing, which can be accomplished by use of material, largely if not entirely existent within my country. My government
will also cooperate with the corporation for suitable employment of the settlers in agricultural work, road building and
other similar activities, it being expected, however, that
the bulk of these first settlers will engage in farming or in
related enterprises. My government will also facilitate and
aid in the transportation of the refugees to my country and
in their reception and care upon their arrival, and in securing appropriate legislation to expedite the carrying forward
of the project herein discussed by appropriate statutes as to
emigration, labor and other laws assuring full civil and
economic rights and safeguards. My government will also
take appropriate steps to aid in the selection of suitable
lands for agricultural purposes and for the acquisition of
such lands by the corporation, either through lease or purchase at fair terms for the benefit of the settlers; and
also the government will further be ready to enter into discussion with the corporation looking toward the giving of
options to the corporation for larger adjacent suitable agricultural lands for later and greater settlement which is
contemplated.

The question of unmarried young men and girls who are
to come with this first group has been given much thought by

177

my government, and I am happy to say that I have been able to make satisfactory arrangements for them. It is my understanding that the corporation to be formed will bring a small number of such young people to my country, and will construct a suitable dormitory, school house and agricultural training grounds for their care, upkeep and education.

Through the intense, humanitarian, benevolent interest of a Dominican patriot, I am confident that arrangements will be made for financing the care of these young people for a period of two years so that they will be able to receive instruction in the religions in which they were born, as well as secular education which will fit them for citizenship in the Dominican Republic, and it is confidently hoped that the future will prove that they will turn out to be valuable acquisitions to our future national life.

The corporation to be formed shall have by appropriate act of our government the right to purchase, lease, acquire or dispose of tracts of land, initiate industries, etc., provided such activities shall be in line with the general governmental policies of my country. We shall encourage the corporation to aid the establishment and development of industries; particularly at the outset, handcraft industries for the settlers.

The corporation is to have the right at its own expense to maintain an adequate, competent technical staff for the

178

guidance of the settlers.

The selection of the settlers shall be recommended by
the corporation but subject to the approval of my government.
The corporation is to make every effort to use in the development of its projects all material, equipment and manpower
which may be available in my country and which shall be
appropriate for its purposes. The corporation is to have the
right to equip and maintain receiving and training camps for
the settlers. Should the corporation acquire lands or
properties, it shall have the right to lease, sell, sublease
or otherwise cede any or all of such properties to the
settlers on terms to be arranged between the corporation and
the settlers. My government will, at all times, assist the
corporation in the selection of all necessary tracts of land
on fair and advantageous terms. The government will permit
the settlers to form purchase, sale or credit group coopera-
tives along such lines as may not be inconsistent with our
general governmental policies. The education facilities,
both in school and university in my government, shall be
available to the settlers on the same conditions as those
which apply to all citizens of my country. The settlers
shall have full right to the protection of our courts and of
the other branches of my government, as have all other citizens of my country.

Based upon this letter, my government is prepared to

179

enter into a definite agreement with the corporation about to
be formed. I understand that you will wish to submit any
such proposed agreement to the President's Advisory Committee,
to Mr. Myron C. Taylor and to the State Department of the
United States for approval. This will be entirely satisfactory to the Dominican Government.

I close with the following statement:

If, with God's blessing, this initial undertaking, modest
though it may be, can succeed, I trust that my country may
have contributed, in collaboration with yours, to the solution
of grave world problems by blazing a path, founded not merely
on humanitarian principles, but on renewed recognition of
the well established fact that the right kind of human material, given a fair opportunity, can and will become important
elements in the upbuilding of countries of immigration. In
his notable address on October 17th, President Roosevelt referred to the vast refugee problems which are daily being aggra-
vated and increased by the exigencies of war and persecution;
and to the vast numbers of human beings whose roots have literally been torn up. He pointed out that there are today, many
vacant spaces on the earth's surface where, from the point
of view of climate and resources, European settlers can live
permanently. I trust that my country can do its share in
pointing the way toward a wise, just and humane solution of
these vast problems, so closely related to world peace. This

my country offers wholeheartedly to do. All the more important will it become that we proceed gradually, seeing to it, step by step, that healthy and sound progress shall be made.

With these thoughts in mind, I am glad that there has been full agreement in the conferences which have led to this letter on the point that the beginning must be on a modest scale. Later steps will depend on many considerations. I emphasize this point, about which we are in full agreement, because we realize that as soon as the work begins and shows progress, there are apt to be early and pressing appeals from unfortunate refugees for the further opening of our doors; appeals to which we shall not wish to be deaf, but which we can meet only in due time.

181

No other arrangements for settlement purposes will be made by my government excepting after conferences and consultations with officials of your organization.

Trusting that this effort which follows the noble initiative of the President of your country may meet with success, I am

Yours very sincerely,

(Signed)
A. PASTORIZA,
Andres Pastoriza,
E.E. and Minister Plenipotentiary.

Mr. Taylor: I think, Mr. Chairman, if I may say so, some special recognition should be given to Mr. McDonald and Mr.

Warren, and the private organizations who have financed and who have carried on this very important study with respect to Dominica. The names of the members of the Commission,- and the one who supervised its organization is Dr. Bowman,- should form a part of our record. Those names can be supplied here-after, if you approve of my suggestion.

Lord Winterton: Should we place it in the record in form something like this, that the Conference hears the suggestion with great satisfaction, and then proceed to mention the names of those gentlemen who contributed to the success of the plan? If that is agreed to, then we will suggest that our Technical Committee, or our experts, draft the actual terms of the reference.

Sir Herbert has suggested to me privately that in that reference in our record we might also mention the Dominican Government.

Mr. Taylor: And General Trujilio.

Lord Winterton: I have the following statement to make in regard to the report of the Technical Committee:

The Technical Committee appointed by the officers of the Intergovernmental Committee for the purpose of preparing a draft communique to be issued after the fourth meeting of the officers scheduled to take place on October 26, 1939, respectfully submits the following text:

Communique

"The officers of the Intergovernmental Committee, at their fourth meeting at Washington, on October 26, 1939, recognized that there was an urgent need for further openings for the permanent settlement of refugees included within the present mandate of the Committee, and further recognized that, as the President of the United States of America pointed out in his inspiring statement of October 17, the problem of involuntary migration might be greatly increased. They considered it necessary that surveys should continue of all possible openings for the permanent settlement of involuntary migrants in various parts of the world, special regards being paid to the scope for the development of natural resources by engineering, irrigation, and similar schemes. While such surveys would have reference to the existing mandate of the Intergovernmental Committee, the meeting observed that the collection of material of this character would be of general value in contributing towards the solution of the refugee problem in its wider aspects, and would be of particular value to the Committee should it at any future time wish to increase the categories of involuntary migrants within its mandate.

183

"The meeting considered that the results of all surveys made either under the aegis of the Coordinating Foundation or by private organizations should be communicated to the

Director, and, at his discretion, to the participating governments."

Gentlemen, Your Excellencies, that proposed communique
has been communicated privately to the heads of all delegations, and I take it we are in agreement that it should be
adopted.

That then disposes of point 6 of the agenda.

We welcome here this afternoon Mr. Van Zeeland, who was
prevented by untoward events in the Atlantic from getting
here the other day, and I would invite Mr. Van Zeeland, if
he will, to address the Conference.

(Applause.)

184

Mr. Paul Van Zeeland: Mr. Chairman, and gentlemen:
There are many aspects of the refugee problem that are so
familiar to you that it would be extremely difficult for a
newcomer like myself to add any light to the problem. The
matter, as I have seen it, has been fully covered and explained, and the situation fully reviewed in the notes which
have been submitted to the Committee. It has been brought
out in these notes that real and considerable achievements
have already been realized in helping refugees to find new
homes, and from a careful reading of the proceedings of your
meeting of last week I have gathered the impression that
your Conference has been able to effectuate a very good
"mise au point" of the problem.

In spite of all that, I let myself be convinced that it would not be useless if I would sum up before you several of the reflections and temporary conclusions which I have been forming after the many contacts I have had on this question in the last period. Of course I will say nothing new, and you will probably think that I am repeating things that you know better than I do, but it seemed to me that it would be useful, in spite of that, for me to come before you and express the views that I have formed in a private capacity.

It appears to me that the problem is to be approached basically as a non-sectarian, non-racial, and non-discriminatory problem, and that the solution to be devised shall be open in the future as in the past to all refugees, irrespective of the cause of their migration.

The war, as has been so duly exposed to you, has brought many changes in the problem. The changes are such that nobody could, safely or accurately, forecast what will happen to this problem at the end of the war; but it seems to me that we can safely accept two views: one of immediate character, and another of long-range theoretical character.

First, that the problem is going on and that the search for a solution must be continued and pushed as strongly and as quickly as possible, and in this connection it becomes, besides your activity, the activity of the private organization and of the Coordinating Foundation.

Secondly, there is a fact that should not be overlooked, and which is, to a certain extent, new. It is that, on the one hand, the world has become legally occupied, and, on the other hand, that migrations of some kind, either purely voluntary, or under social pressure, or again under economic pressure, not to mention the political pressure, are a constant fact in history, and are probably a necessary element for the maintenance of a social and economic equilibrium in the world. If that is so, the necessity of devising ways and means for an orderly kind of migration is due to retain the attention of the leaders.

186

When it comes to the actual problem of refugees I maintain that it presents two different aspects which are, of course, closely related and which react upon one another, but which should be clearly distinguished. The first is the problem of upkeep, maintenance, and relief of the refugees in the way of migration, and the other is the definite settlement of the refugees in new, permanent conditions of life.

Of course the necessity of keeping alive the refugees in migration until they are definitely established cannot be disputed in any way, but let us not forget for a moment that if a constructive scheme for a new, permanent settlement on a certain scale would receive an actual beginning of execution, the prospects opened by it would react so as to facilitate the actual solution of many questions concerning the relief and the transitory asylum of the refugees.

Not being mandated to speak for my country here, I will just say, in passing, that it covers the question which you have, in my opinion, very clearly covered, I mean the special situation of the small neutral countries in Europe such as Holland, Switzerland, Sweden, and Belgium, where so many temporary refugees are waiting for a definite solution of their difficulties.

So we come to the necessity of expediting the definitive settlement of the refugees. The pressure is such that no method whatsoever, small or large, quick or slow, for obtaining that purpose could, in my opinion, be neglected or set aside.

187

All methods to settle people definitely somewhere should have recourse to, concurrently, I will mention first, infiltration and the use of every possible opportunity for individual settlement in old or new countries in Europe or elsewhere, in the United States or in Palestine, in the neutral countries or Europe or in the newer countries of South America. All administrative facilities should be continued as they have been in the past, sought for, and extended as far as possible. But I think we may recognize the fact that even all that would not be sufficient, and that finally all possibilities for the establishment of new settlements anywhere in the world on any scale, big or small should be examined and studied and promoted as quickly as possible.

This method of new settlements commends itself for many reasons in addition to the one that has just been invoked. Its use will facilitate and enlarge continuation of infiltration in countries where otherwise fears of saturation might arise more quickly. It will facilitate also the continuation of the liberal attitude of the countries of temporary asylum. But above all,- if I may here just touch an aspect which, in my eyes, is very important, above all, new settlements, if successful, and if made in accordance with sound economic principles, might, at a certain stage, be considered as one of the many elements which will be required at a certain time in order to reorganize again on a sounder basis the economic life of the world.

188

But of course the establishment of new settlers on any scale in any country must, to be successful, reflect a series of rules and principles arising out of numerous past experiences, be these experiences successful or unsuccessful.

It seems to me that good ideas might be found in the study of the relative or excellent successes achieved in several circumstances by the formulae of more or less autonomous territories.

The possibility of creating, for definite economic purposes, privileged international companies has already been

emphasized in several international meetings or conferences.
The possibilities inherent in such privileged companies, so
far as refugee settlements are concerned, should, in my
opinion, be carefully examined and eventually utilized.

From modern developments in the technique of production,
it seems to me that in the beginning new settlements should
be established, not exclusively but principally upon agriculture on a subsistence basis. Immediately after that, at a
very early date, small industries, especially related either
to the immediate needs of the community and/or the use of
agricultural products should be and could be envisaged. It
should not be forgotten that the new methods of transportation for man and for power render possible the establishment
of semi-urban agglomerations which can be made consistent
with semi-agricultural life, under certain conditions of
climate and soil.

189

But immediately comes to your mind the question of financing. If I have insisted so much upon the necessity of
distinguishing between the two aspects of the problem, of
relief and maintenance on the one hand, and permanent settlement on the other, it is because this distinction applies, in
my opinion, duly to conclusions as far as financing is concerned.

In the first case, obviously, it is charity which must
come to the top and the money must be brought in by strong

appeals to humanitarian and charitable purposes.

On the contrary, the question of permanent settlement should be considered, treated, and solved, at least to a very large extent, on an economic basis. I know some of the difficulties of such a proposal. I know that this opinion does not meet with unqualified approval; but it seems to me that it is both in the moral and material interests of the refugees as a whole that the approach to this part of the problem should be made, as far as possible, on an economic basis. This brings with it many conclusions. First, it means that the sums put at the disposal of the refugees for permanent settlement will not be given but loaned to them -- and here comes the very important problem of interest or no interest. On the other hand, it means that the formulae to be adopted for raising the money should be based upon the investment idea, at least to a limited or definite extent. There are precedents in history, but they do not apply exactly to our circumstances. So new formulae should be evolved. It would take some imagination and also especially the collaboration of prominent people in business life, but from the studies already made I have gathered the definite impression that most of the objections usually made against the approach of that problem could relatively easily and practically be met. It is not the time nor the place to go into any details, but from what I have heard and studied I would be very

190

surprised if satisfactory formulae could not be devised by
practical business men.

Now the most important point is that rapidly a beginning
of concrete realization is reached. It would not matter, in
my opinion, if this beginning were very small, provided the
direction chosen and the concept of the scheme are such that
it might duly expand in accordance with circumstances, neces-
sities and possibilities.

I have been very gratified in learning of the progress
that has been made in some of the schemes under review: the
Dominican Republic scheme in particular, and the Philippine
scheme, but, generally speaking, it seems to me that to
hasten practical achievements a few requirements should be
desirable.

191

First, that a certain unity of action, or at least some
centralization, in some form of the many private efforts
that are being made, and sometimes so successfully made,
should be obtained. Of course it lies in the scope of
effort of the Coordinating Foundation.

Second, it seems to me that it should be necessary to
the greatest possible extent, to utilize all the competencies
which have in the past, even in the remote past, or in the
last circumstances, affirmed or reaffirmed themselves in any
way, so as to get together all the good will possible.

And finally, I think it will surprise nobody if I insist
upon the desirability, and I should say the necessity, of the

leadership in these circumstances of the United States of America. The generous and successful initiatives taken by President Roosevelt in this matter; the fact that the war is requiring the best energies of all citizens in the big countries in Europe; the thought also that in all large humanitarian and economic problems the United States people have always taken the most important share, all these things point clearly, as I said, to the desirability and maybe the necessity of the United States taking not only the actual burden but also the eventual reward, either moral or material, of such a magnificent enterprise.

192

Mr. Chairman and gentlemen, the Coordinating Foundation, of which I have accepted temporarily to direct the efforts, has, it seems to me, under the circumstances, as one of its primary duties, to help studying, centralizing, and realizing settlements of refugees in new places. The Foundation will have especially to find out whether and how the capital necessary to carry out such a huge enterprise can be raised. We have come to a point which might well prove to be a true crossroads. The few contacts I have had since my arrival here do not allow me to express any forecast as to the immediate possibility, but at least they have left me with a definite impression that there is here a will to come to broad achievements, and this seems to me enough to justify new and greater hopes, because,— and this will close these

few remarks,- I am fully convinced that, according to the
proverb, "Where there is a will there is a way."

(Applause.)

Lord Winterton: Gentlemen, I should like to say on
behalf of all of us, how fortunate we are to have associated,
through his connection with the Foundation as President, so
eminent a person as Mr. Van Zeeland.

Mr. Taylor: Mr. Chairman, I should like to associate
our Government with the Chairman's observation in respect to
Mr. Van Zeeland. I think that, in the character of our
organization, representing as we do, as I constantly repeat,
thirty-two governments in the present world unrest, with the
cooperation of the Foundation which must represent a great
body of opinion, not only opinion but the willingness or the
ability to lend actual service to this cause, that we are
vigilant and active, and contribute in a real way to the solution of the problems which are bound to arise in the very
near future. So I hope, Mr. Chairman, that the full power
and authority of the Intergovernmental Committee will be
invoked under all circumstances in which they can be of use
and service, because I believe that this question is one
segment, one very important segment, in the unrest of the
world of today.

Lord Winterton: Does any other delegate wish to speak

193

on Mr. van Zeeland's statement?

(No response.)

Lord Winterton: Then we will pass to the next business, which is the designation of a Secretary of the Committee.

When the Intergovernmental Conference took place we were fortunate in having, as our Secretary at that Conference, M. Jean Paul-Boncour of the French Foreign Office, and I might mention at the private dinner which was given to Mr. Taylor the other night I expressed my appreciation of M. Paul-Boncour's work. When that committee was constituted as a permanent body, following the Conference, Mr. Roger Makins of the Foreign Office was designated Secretary, and he also did most valuable work for the committee. About Christmas of last year, owing to his removal to another department of the Foreign Office, of our Foreign Office, it was no longer possible for him to continue as Secretary, and consequently Mr. Reilly of the British Foreign Office was appointed Secretary, and he in turn had to resign the secretaryship at the outbreak of the present war, because his service is required in another department of the government in our country, and Mr. Warr of the British Foreign Office was appointed as acting secretary. It was, however, represented to us, through the United States Embassy in London to the Foreign Office, that it would be probably convenient, for the purpose of this Conference if Mr. Morris took Mr. Warr's place as acting secretary.

Now the Secretary of the Committee is designated by the
Chairman under our constitution after consultation with and
agreement by two of the Vice-Chairmen, and although this Conference has no executive authority, which is vested in the
whole Committee, it would seem to me to be a convenient
occasion for designating a permanent Secretary instead of the
acting secretary which we have at present. After consultation with and the approval of my colleagues of this Conference, the French Ambassador, and Mr. Myron Taylor, I
designate Mr. Morris as the Secretary of our Committee.
Mr. Morris has the advantage, which few of us around this
table possess, with one or two exceptions, of being a young
man who is already much interested in the work of the
Committee, and I am sure he will fill this post which has
been so admirably filled in the past, with equal facility and
felicity. I have pleasure in designating Mr. Morris as
Secretary.

195

(Applause.)

Lord Winterton: The next business is important also,
and that is the designation of a Vice-Director to replace Mr.
Joseph Harsh, resigned. Mr. Harsh was appointed Vice-
Director for a term only. He gave valuable assistance to
the Director in London, as Sir Herbert will tell you in a
moment. He came originally on the understanding that his

services would be only required for a comparatively limited period, as he has other work to do. In fact we were allowed to make use of his services owing to permission given to him by a great newspaper which employs him, to leave the work of that newspaper for a short time in order to assist this Committee. The post is, therefore, at present vacant. I will ask Sir Herbert Emerson, if he will, to make some remarks on this matter.

Sir Herbert Emerson: I should like to associate myself with the remarks made by the Chairman regarding the services rendered by Mr. Harsch during the time he was Vice-Director. We had hoped to retain his services until April of next year, but it was a condition of the terms imposed by the newspaper, on which he is permanently employed, that if war broke out he should return to his post. When war began he had to leave the Committee, and I believe he is now busy reporting the events of the war.

I think it is very necessary to have a Vice-Director who will generally assist the Director and in his absence will be responsible for the executive action of the Committee. The suggestion has been made that in making that appointment it would be of value if someone was selected who was a national of one of the neutral countries of Europe, and I think myself. especially in view of the importance attaching to economic investigations and inquiries, that in looking for such a man we should attempt to find one who had had practical training as an economist, and, if possible, some technical experience. At the moment I do not think we have anyone particularly in mind whom I could recommend to the Chairman for appointment, but if the suggestion commends itself to the officer I would, in looking for a suitable candidate bear these qualifications in mind and make corresponding recommendations to the Chairman.

Mr. Taylor: Mr. Chairman, I hope, in making the selection, you will not be governed by any consideration of economy, and I hope that you will select the most outstanding person that is available, because the service that he can render to Sir Herbert, to you, and to this Committee, is almost beyond imagination.

197

Lord Winterton: Speaking for myself, I should like to say that I personally would like to see some such appointment as the kind Sir Herbert suggested be made. I think it would be of great value, for many reasons, if we could have a national of one of the countries which he mentioned appointed.

The next business is the financial position of the Committee. I invite our Director to report certain facts in connection therewith.

Sir Herbert Emerson: There is very little to report since the full meeting of the Committee took place in the middle of July last. Certain arrears have been collected.

Canada has paid her arrears in full. A contribution has been received from the French Government and another also from Mexico. The expenses have been normal, and at the end of August, when the last balance sheet was returned by the bank, the Committee was in funds approximately to the sum of £2,400.

At the outbreak of war the expenditure was cut down to the minimum possible. The office of the Vice-Director remained temporarily in abeyance. Several of the employees were given notice that their services would no longer be required, and owing to the uncertainty about office conditions in London, and owing to the kindness of the Office of Works, we were able to get rid of the liability we then had for considerable office rent. It will be necessary to take some office accommodation in London, but on a smaller scale than previously, but at the moment, and taking into account the contribution which the Government of the United States makes, I do not think there is any anxiety for the future, for the immediate future at any rate, as the Committee is in sufficient funds to carry on without difficulty, at any rate for the next year.

Lord Winterton: Now, Your Excellencies, that concludes our business, unless any delegate has any other matter which he wishes to bring up. If not, I should like, as Chairman of the Conference, to ask my colleagues to pay some tribute, first,

to the President of the United States for his action in
calling this Conference; secondly, to the State Department
for all the arrangements that they have made for our comfort
and convenience, and for their very material assistance
towards what has been, I think, a useful and fruitful
Conference.

I should like to say to their excellencies, the delegates, that it has been both an honor and pleasure to me to
preside over our deliberations. Some of us have met in
connection with the business of this Committee constantly in
different places. We have sat around tables during our discussions in Evian, on several occasions in London, and now
in the State Department; and others have been at the Conference in connection with the Committee for the first time.
Some of us who have met here for the first time have had
connections at other places. Perhaps I might mention the
interesting fact that the French Ambassador, during the last
war, visited a portion of the line in the battle on the plains
of Gaza, visited a company in a battalion of which I was
second in command, and spoke to a brother officer of mine who
was killed shortly afterward, who had been a very great friend
of mine and who was second in command of that particular
company when I commanded it -- a rather interesting fact.

Well, I would like to say, in conclusion, that I hope
we may all be associated in the future in this or some
other work of value to humanity at large, because I think

199

we can say without conceit that all the nations represented around this table have made and can make a great contribution to that end.

Count de Saint-Quentin: I want to second the Chairman's remarks in expressing thanks to the President of the United States who once more takes leadership in a great and generous international cause that is so useful to our world and our civilization.

I also want to express my thanks to the State Department. The State Department, on every occasion, is very helpful and obliging, and now they have given us once more proof of it.

I want to thank Lord Winterton for his kind words in his reference to me, and for his recollections in regard to our previous meeting. It is true that I was near Gaza at the same time that he was there, and one of the great problems that confronted us was the Palestine refugee problem.

I remember the fact that I saw the second of the line where he was in command, and once more, on that day, I received a very hearty welcome from his second in command, and I also thank him for the cup of chocolate. It was very welcome, because it was very chilly in the plains of Gaza.

Mr. Taylor: Mr. Chairman, I wish on behalf of your host, the Government of the United States and President Roosevelt, to thank you and the other delegates who are assembled here in respect to this very important question,

200

and I thank you for the interest you have taken and the skill that you have shown in the conduct of these proceedings.

Lord Winterton: We are much obliged to hear your very kind words, and for myself I feel, and I am sure Sir Herbert does, that our journey, possibly a somewhat hazardous journey across the Atlantic, was fully justified by the importance of the matters we have discussed here, and especially by the contacts which our eminent directors have been able to make with so many of the individuals and associations in this country in connection with the refugee problem.

If there is nothing further the Conference will adjourn.

(Whereupon, at the hour of 4 o'clock p.m., the Conference adjourned.)

201

Abschrift !

Geheime Staatspolizei   Berlin, den 31.Januar 1939
Geheimes Staatspolizeiamt
II D Allg. Nr.38 298

> An
>   alle Staatspolizeileit- und -stellen,
>   die Referate der Abteilungen II und III
>   (ohne Grenzinspekteure)
>
> <u>Nachrichtlich</u>
> an
>   den Führer der ℋ-Totenkopfstandarten und
>   Konzentrationslager in Oranienburg
>   (mit 8 Überdrucken für die Lager).

<u>Betrifft</u>: Entlassung von jüdischen Schutzhäftlingen.

    Der Reichsführer ℋ und Chef der Deutschen Polizei hat ent-
schieden,

1) daß jüdische Rassenschänder ebenfalls aus der Schutzhaft entlassen
werden können, wenn sie sonst in politischer und krimineller Hin-
sicht <u>nicht</u> in Erscheinung getreten sind <u>und auswandern wollen.</u>

Doc. 9

202

2) daß als Stichtag für die Anordnung betreffend Verbot jeglichen
Waffenbesitzes für Juden der 20.11.38 festgelegt wird.

    Hierzu verweise ich auf die Presseveröffentlichungen vom
10.11.38, wonach Personen, die nach den Nürnberger Gesetzen als
Juden gelten, jeglicher Waffenbesitz verboten ist und Zuwider-
handelnde in Konzentrationslager übergeführt und auf die Dauer
von 20 Jahren in Schutzhaft zu nehmen sind.
    Falls es sich bei den aufgefundenen Waffen um Hiebwaffen
(Säbel und Degen), oder auch alte Feuerwaffen handelt, die lediglich als Andenken an die Militär- bezw. Kriegszeit zu be-
trachten sind, können diese gegebenenfalls den Juden belassen
werden.

3) jüdische Schutzhäftlinge können grundsätzlich, wenn sie im Besitz
von Auswanderungspapieren für andere europäische Staaten -- also
nicht nur nach Übersee -- sind, entlassen werden.

4) Die mündliche Androhung der lebenslänglichen Überführung in ein
Konzentrationslager, falls der Betreffende, der zum Zwecke der Auswanderung aus der Schutzhaft entlassen worden ist, später unerlaubt
zurückkehrt, hat weiterhin in jedem Falle zu erfolgen.

- - - - - -

    Ich gebe von dieser Anordnung des Reichsführers ℋ und Chefs
der Deutschen Polizei Kenntnis und ersuche, die Schutzhaftvorgänge
entsprechend zu überprüfen und sofern die vollständigen Unterlagen
zur Auswanderung beigebracht/sind, unter Beiziehung der Lagerbeurtei-
                       worden/
lung im Einzelfalle zu berichten.

                                         Soweit

Soweit es sich bei den Häftlingen um frühere kommunistische Funktionäre, insbesondere um führende Intellektuelle handelt, deren Entlassung auch zum Zwecke der Auswanderung nicht angängig erscheint, bitte ich, dies in den Berichten unter Anführung der Bedenken, die einer Entlassung zwecks Auswanderung entgegenstehen, besonders hervorzuheben.

Die unter 4 aufgeführte mündliche Androhung ist wie bisher bereits in Einzelfällen angeordnet, auch ohne besondere Weisung weiterhin vorzunehmen.

Dieser Erlaß ist nicht für die Orts- und Kreispolizeibehörden bestimmt.

Zusatz für die Staatspolizeileitstelle Wien:

Falls es sich um Häftlinge handelt, bei denen Schutzhaft von hier noch nicht angeordnet worden ist, ersuche ich, entsprechend diesen Richtlinien in eigener Zuständigkeit zu verfahren bezw. in jedem Einzelfalle die hiesige Entscheidung einzuholen.

Über alle Häftlinge, die in eigener Zuständigkeit entlassen werden, sind jedoch nachträglich Entlassungsmitteilungen, die im Abzugsverfahren hergestellt werden können, für jeden einzelnen Häftling nach folgendem Muster nach hier einzureichen:

Personalien:
Tag der Festnahme:
Grund der Festnahme:
Ort der Unterbringung:
Tag der Entlassung:
Wann und wohin ausgewandert;

                    gez.: H e y d r i c h

    (Siegel)   Beglaubigt:
                    gez.:Unterschrift
                    Kanzleiangestellte

Geheime Staatspolizei   Düsseldorf,den 13.Februar 1939
Staatspolizeistelle
  -Düsseldorf-
II B 4/71^{02}/247/39

            An
               die Außendienststellen
               und die Dienststellen II A und II D im Hause

Abschrift übersende ich zur gefl.Kenntnis und Beachtung.-

            Im Auftrage:
               gez.:Humpert   Beglaubigt:

                                    Pol.Büro-Asst.

EMBASSY OF THE
UNITED STATES OF AMERICA
No. 621   Berlin, March 8, 1939

Subject: Emigration Levy Imposed by the
          Central Jewish Organization in
          Germany.

The Honorable

     A-M/The Secretary of State,
     RECORDING DESK
     FILE-C.S.   Washington.

Sir:

          I have the honor to enclose a translation of
an order issued by the Reich Association of Jews in
Germany, which is the officially recognized central
Jewish organization, imposing, with the approval of
the Reich Government authorities, an emigration levy
upon departing Jewish emigrants whose property exceeds RM 1,000 in value.

          This levy is to be collected by the competent
branch offices of the Reich Association or by the
various Jewish religious communities themselves, and
it is understood that these recognized Jewish organizations will be empowered to administer and spend

                                                  the

Doc. 10

204

the proceeds for their work among the Jews in Germany.
The levy is to be paid in addition to the government
capital flight tax and in a certain sense represents
a self-imposed tax, it being felt that it is only
fair that the Jews who are leaving should make a contribution to the communities to enable the latter to
carry on their welfare activities, as well as to assist poorer Jews in emigrating. Although confirma-
tion is lacking, it is understood that the levy will
be assessed on a scale varying from one to eight per
cent of the emigrant's property. The tax will evi-
dently be officially enforced to the extent that the
final papers for departure will not be issued until
after payment has been certified.

205

2/   As of possible interest I also enclose copies
of the forms which Jews desiring to emigrate must
now submit to the competent Reich exchange offices.
It will be observed that the questionnaires envisage
remarkably complete answers regarding property owned
by such Jews, the prospective emigrant, for example,
being required to list his personal belongings, such
as shirts, etc., piece by piece. Owing to the lengthy
nature of these forms it has been found impossible to
render an English translation.

        There is enclosed finally, as a separate annex,
the most recent issue of the JÜDISCHES NACHRICHTEN-
BLATT which is the only paper the Jews are now permitted to publish following the suppression of their

                                        various

various periodicals last November, and which is important as the only source of information covering certain types of decrees and notices affecting the Jews.   Attention is invited to the back page (page 16) of this copy where several advertisements will be found offering for sale preferred positions on the waiting list for American immigration visas. As soon as this was brought to my attention, I requested the editor of the publication to call upon me and informed him that such an exchange of places on the waiting list could only be effected by fraud.   He promised me that hereafter no further advertisements of this nature would be accepted or printed.

206

Respectfully yours,

Raymond H. Geist
Chargé d'Affaires ad interim

Enclosures:
1. Translation of an order published in JÜDISCHES NACHRICHTENBLATT of March 3, 1939.
2. Copies of Questionnaires for Jewish emigrants.
3. Recent issue of JÜDISCHES NACHRICHTENBLATT.

804.4

JDB:EM

Enclosure No. 2 to despatch
No. 621, dated March 8, 19 3 9
from the American Embassy,
Berlin, Germany.

(COPY)

F r a g e b o g e n für jüdische Auswanderer

Dieser Fragebogen ist nur von Juden deutscher Staatsangehörigkeit und von staatenlosen Juden Auszufullen.

Anmerkung: Der Fragebogen ist vollständig ausgefüllt und unterschrieben
mit einem schriftlichen Antrag und den bei den Fragen be-
zeichneten Unterlagen mindestens 3 Wochen vor Verpackung und
Verladung des Umzugsgutes der Devisenstelle Berlin einzureichen. Anträge bei denen ausreichende Unterlagen fehlen, bzw.
bei denen der Fragebogen unvollständig ausgefüllt ist, müssen
kurzerhand zurückgegeben werden. Das Beantworten der einzelnen Fragen durch Einsetzen von Strichen ist unzulässig.

1. Name des Auswanderers:
2. Geburtsdatum: Ort:
3. Sind Sie ledig, verheiratet, verwitwet, geschieden?
4. Welche Personen wandern mit Ihnen aus? (Ehefrau.Kinder, sonstige Angehörige,genaue Angaben sind erforderlich: (vergl.Punk
L-4)

5. Sind Verwandte in auf- oder absteigender Linie seit dem 3.8.
1931 ausgewandert und wohin? Oder sind von diesen in letzter
Zeit Auswanderungsanträge gestellt worden? Gegebenenfalls sin
Namen und letzte inländische Anschriften aufzuführen.

6. Haben Sie bereits einen Antrag auf Mitnahme von Umzugsgut,
Reisegepäck usw.bei einer Devisenstelle gestellt? Gegebenenfalls bei welcher Devisenstelle?

7. Wohin wollen Sie auswandern?
8. Wann werden Sie voraussichtlich Deutschland verlassen?
Bei welcher Schiffahrtsgesellschaft wird gegebenenfalls die
Schiffskarte gelöst?
9. Welchen Beruf haben Sie bisher gehabt,oder waren Sie selbst-
ständig und in welchem Geschäftszweig?
10. Wollen Sie Ihren bisherigen Beruf im Ausland ausüben oder
beabsichtigen Sie einen anderen Beruf zu ergreifen?
11. Welche Staatsangehörigkeit haben Sie?
Falls Ausländer a) seit wann sind Sie in Deutschland ansässi
b) verlassen Sie Deutschland auf Grund eines
polizeilichen Ausweisungsbefehles?
12. Seit wann haben Sie Ihren ständigen Wohnsitz in Berlin,bzw.
wo haben Sie seit dem 3.8.1931 gewohnt?
13. Welches Einkommen haben Sie gehabt: 1936?_____RM
1937? RM_____   1938?_____RM
14. An welches Steueramt und unter welcher Steuernummer haben
Sie Ihre Steuern bisher abgeführt?
15. Welche Vermögenswerte wollen Sie neben dem Umzugsgut ausfüh-
ren?
16. Welches Vermögen versteuerten Sie nach dem Vermögenssteuer-
bescheid vom 1.Januar 1936 RM_____welches Vermögen
Sie besitzen Sie heute? RM_____
(Als besondere Anlage ist eine genaue Vermögensaufstellun
beizufügen.In der Vermögensausstellung sind sämtliche
Wertpapiere,Grundbesitz,Bankguthaben,Forderungen,Versich-
erungen usw.einzeln zu verzeichnen.Ihre Gläubiger sind
einzeln zu benennen).

207

17. In meinem bezw.unserem (siehe Ziffer 5) Eigentum befindet
    sich Schmuck im Werte von RM_____laut beiliegender
    Aufstellung und Taxe

18. Welches Vermögen versteuern Ihre Eltern? RM_____

19. Welches Vermögen versteuern Ihre Schwiegereltern? RM_____

20. Haben Sie zwecks Beschaffung der Mittel zur Auswanderung Dar-
    lehen aufgenommen oder Schenkungen,Abfindungen etc.erhalten,
    wenn ja von wem und in welcher Höhe? (ganaue Anschrift ist
    erforderlich)

21. Ich erkläre ausdrücklich:
    a) Ich habe keinerlei Forderungen gegen Ausländer (Export-
       und Kapitalforderungen).
    b) Ich bin an keiner Firma beteiligt,die Exportgeschäfte be-
       treibtö
    c) Ich besitze weder mittelbar noch unmittelbar irgendwelche
       Patent-,Urheber-,Vertriebs-oder ähnliche Rechte.
       (Falls Sie diese Erklärung nicht abgeben können,haben Sie
       auf einer besonderen Anlage Ihre sämtlichen Forderungen
       gegen Ausländer,Ihre Beteilungen an in-und ausländischen
       Firmen,sowie die obenbezeichneten Rechte einzeln aufzu-
       führen).

22. Hiermit erkläre ich,dass ich Schulden gegenüber inländischen
    Gläubigern nicht habe, dass mein nach der Auswanderung im
    Inland (Deutschland) verbleibendes Vermögen zur Befriedigung
    meiner inländischen Gläubiger ausreicht. (Aufstellung der
    Schulden gegen inländische Gläubiger anliegend. (Fehlanzeige
    erforderlich)

    Die Richtigkeit und Vollständigkeit meiner Angaben versichere
    ich nach besten Wissen und Gewissen.Die Strafbestimmungen
    §§ 69 ff. des Dev.Ges.vom 12.12.1938 sind mir bekannt.

                    Berlin,_____

                    _____
                    (Unterschrift des Auswanderers)

                    Wohnort:_____

                    Strasse u.Hausnr._____

(EM)

(COPY)

Centralstelle für jüdische Auswanderung,Berlin, W.62,
(Devissenstelle)-

M e r k b l a t t

für die Mitnahme von Umzugsgut und sonstigen Sachen
durch jüdische Auswanderer.

Gemäss § 57 des Devisengesetzes vom 12.Dezember 1938 dürfen
Auswanderer Umzugsgut und sonstige Sachen nur mit Genehmigung ins
Ausland versenden oder überbringen. Anträge auf Genehmigung sind
mindestens 3 Wochen vor der Verpackung und Verladung zu stellen.
Erst nach Erteilung der devisenrechtlichen Genehmigung gemäss § 57
des Devisengesetzes dürfen Umzugsgüter und sonstige Sachen jüdischer
Auswanderer von den Spediteuren auf Lager genommen oder zum Versand
gebracht werden.

Dem Antrag sind folgende Unterlagen beizufügen:

1.   Der beiliegende Fragebogen (Vordruck 421a); ist
ausgefüllt und vom Auswanderer eigenhändig unterschrieben in
doppelter Ausfertigung einzureichen.

2. Ein genaues Verzeichnis der zur Ausfuhr bestimmten Gegenstände in
dreifacher Ausfertigung (s. umstehendes Muster). Es ist hierbei
zu beachten,dass unter allen Umständen Gegenstände, die vor dem
1.Januar 1933 angeschafft worden sind,von solchen Gegenständen,
die nach dem 1.Januar 1933 erworben worden sind, getrennt aufgeführt werden.
Wichtig: Die einzelnen Posten sind fortlaufend zu numerieren!

Es ist unzulässig,im Umzugsgutverzeichnis Sammelbegriffe wie
"Tafelgeschirr" oder "1 Posten Wäsche" usw.anzugeben. Erforderlich sind genaue Angaben: 6 Oberhemden,8 Tischtücher, 24 Mund-
tücher usw. Bei Pelzen ist die Einkaufsrechnung beizufügen, des-
gleichen bei Photoapparaten.

Als Umzugsgut sind anzusehen: Möbel,Wäsche,Kleider,Teppiche(sofern es sich nicht um wertvolle Stücke handelt) und sonstige
Einrichtungsgegenstände. Bei Kühlschränken, Radioapparaten,
Schreibmaschinen,Klavieren,Sprechapparaten,usw. sind im Umzugsgutverzeichnis stets die Fabrikationsnummern diser Gegenstände
und die Markenbezeichnung anzugeben.

3. Eine Aufstellung der Reisegepäcks ebenfalls in dreifacher Aus-
fertigung (s.umstehendes Muster).
Handgepäck kann gemäss § 58 des Devisengesetzes ohne besondere
Genehmigung im Reiseverkehr mitgeführt werden,soweit die in
Frage kommenden Gegenstände unbedings zum persönlichen Gebrauch
während der Reise erforderlich sind.

Zur besonderen Beachtung!!

1. Nicht zum Umzugsgut gehören: Gewerbliche Maschinen,Automobile,
Briefmarken- und Münzsammlungen,wertvolle Gemälde und Antiqui-
täten und sonstige zum Wiederverkauf geeignete Gegenstände.Für
die nicht unter den Begriff "Umzugsgut" fallenden Gegenstände
sind besondere Verzeichnisse in dreifacher Ausfertigung einzu-
reichen.Die Industrie-und Handelskammer macht jüdischen Auswan-
deren vereidigte sachverständige namhaft,die die fraglichen
Gegenstände abschätzen und ein entsprechendes Gutachten erstatten
    Auf dieses Gutachten der vereidigten Sachverständihen der
    Industrie- und Handelskammer kann nur verzichtet werden,wenn
    es sich nachweisbar (Einkaufsrechnungen usw.) um Gegenstände
    von geringem Wert handelt,die vor den 1.1.1933 angeschafft wor-
    den sind(z.b.ärzliches Instrumentarium).

209

2. <u>Anträge auf Genehmigung zur Ausfuhr vorstehender Gegenstände
sind unbedingt gleichzeitig mit dem Antrage auf Genehmigung
zur Ausfuhr des Umzugsgutes und des Reisegepäcks zu stellen.
Nachanträge sind nicht zulässig.</u>

3. Über die Mitnahme von Schmuck und Wertsachen, z.B. Trauringe,
Uhren, Tafelsilber, sind die von der Industrie- und Handelskammer namhaft gemachten vereidigten Sachverständigen unterrichtet.

4. Die Bearbeitung der Anträge auf Mitnahme des Umzugsgutes und
sonstiger Sachen erfolgt mit tunlichster Beschleunigung. <u>Es ist
daher zwecklos,eine Rückfrage zu halten.</u>

Muster des Umzugsgut- Verzeichnisses
Reisegepäck-
(in dreifacher Ausfertigung einzureichen).

Name des Auswanderers
und genaue Anschrift: _____

_____

1 fd. Nr.	Stück Gegenstände (genaue Bezeichnung)	Zeitpunkt der Anschaffung	Einkaufspreis RM.
1.			
2.			
3.			
4.			
5.			

210

(IX)

Translation
from
JÜDISCHES NACHRICHTENBLATT
March 3, 1939.

Imposition of an Emigrants' Tax.

The Reich Association of Jews in Germany states
as follows:

With the permission of the competent authorities
a uniform tax will be imposed upon all Jews (Section 5 of
the First Decree to the Reich Citizen Law) resident in
Germany (Old Reich) in case they emigrate, if their property exceeds 1000 RM; this tax is an emigrants' tax and
will be imposed immediately.   The purpose of this emigrants' tax is to raise funds with which the Reich Association of Jews in Germany may fulfill its duties.

The imposition of this tax is uniform and in
accordance with directives which have already been sent
to the Jewish religious communities. In accordance
therewith, a statement must be presented prior to emigration showing that the emigrant has complied with his
regular obligations towards the Jewish religious community where he has his domicile and has paid the emigrants' tax.   The same applies to preliminary trips
(Informationsreisen).

The emigrants' tax is fixed by the district
office of the Reich Association or Jewish religious
community according to the following local partition:

(Here follows a list of cities and the corresponding offices)

211

In

In order to avoid delay in carrying through emigration, an application must therefore be made in good time prior to the date of emigration to have the amount of the emigrants' tax fixed in accordance with the local partition given above.

AC:EM

212

Enclosure No.3 to despatch
No.3 to despatch No.621 of
March 8, 1939.from American
Embassy,Berlin.

213

A.A.eing. - 6. MAI 1939 Vm

Deutsche Gesandtschaft
Sofia

B 1272/39.
1 Anlage.
3 Doppel.

Sofia, den 3.Mai 1939.

—————— Anliegend übersende ich abschriftlich einen Bericht des
Konsulats Burgas über die Ausreise jüdischer Emigranten nach
Palästina zur gefälligen Kenntnisnahme.

Doc. 11

214

An das
Auswärtige Amt
B e r l i n.

83-26

Deutsches Konsulat
Tageb.Nr.249/39 A.

Burgas,den 28.4.1939.

Im Zusammenhange mit den Meldungen des deutschen Nach-
richtendienstes über illegale Landungen jüdischer Emigranten in
Palästina dürfte es die Gesandtschaft interessieren,dass am 20.d.Mts.
der griechische Dampfer ATIOS NIKOLA den Hafen von Burgas mit etwa
350 Juden aus der Slowakei und Ungarn verlassen hat,um diese nach
Palästina zu bringen. Trotzdem eine Einreisegenehmigung seitens der
Mandatsbehörden nicht erteilt werden konnte,haben die Engländer
sicherm Vernehmen nach eine stillschweigende Duldung der illegalen
Landung an unbewachten Küstenstellen zugesagt. Unter den Passagieren
befinden sich etwa 350 Männer,ausschliesslich militärgediente Leute,
die nach glaubwürdigen Aeusserungen eine den britischen Behörden
willkomene Ergänzung der jüdischen Polizeitruppe darstellen,und etwa
30 Frauen, Das Alter der Männer dürfte durchweg 20 bis 25 Jahre
betragen.

Wie ich heute weiterhin erfuhr,wurde der Dampfer Atios
Nikola inzwischen in einem griechischen Hafen durch die Behörden fest-
gehalten,da angeblich die Dokumente der Reisenden nicht in Ordnung
waren. Gleichzeitig sei allen griechischen Schiffsführern durch
Runderlass unter Androhung des Patentverlustes untersagt worden,
künftig derartige Transporte zu übernehmen.

Atios Nicola ist ein kleiner Dampfer ältester Bauart,der
keinerlei Einrichtungen zur Unterbringung von Passagieren hat. Die-
selben sind in den Lagerräumen auf Holzpritschen notdürftig unterge-
bracht. Rettungs- und sanitäre Einrichtungen dürften kaum für die
Besatzung ausreichend sein. Für die Ueberfahrt von Burgas nach Palästina erhielt der Kapitän,der den Transport angeblich auf eigene Hand
veranstaltet hat,pro Person die aussergewöhnlich hohe Summe von
13.000 Lewa.

Der lange Aufenthalt des D. Atios Nicola von 14 Tagen in
Burgas hat sich bei der bulgarischen Bevölkerung stimmungsmässig
für Deutschland nicht günstig ausgewirkt,da die zahlreichen untätig
in den Cafés herumsitzenden jüdischen Emigranten ausgiebig die
schlimmste Greuelpropaganda betrieben haben.

gez.: Jakubowski.

An die
Deutsche Gesandtschaft
S o f i a .

215

REICHSSTELLE FÜR DAS   BERLIN NW 7, den 5.Oktober 1939.
AUSWANDERUNGSWESEN   Dorotheenstr.49/52.
G.Z.: B 1324/30.8.39

An das
     Auswärtige Amt
     Kult B

      B e r l i n

Auf den wieder beigefügten Erlaß
     vom 29.8.39.
Betrifft: Vermittler von Visa für
     auswanderungswillige Juden.
Berichterstatter: Ministerialrat
     Dr.Müller.

[Stempel: Auswärtiges Amt 83-24 5/10 eing. OKT. 1939]

Die Anfrage des Herrn Reichswirtschaftsministers wird
nebst Beilagen mit nachfolgender Stellungnahme zurückgereicht:

Viele Juden suchen ihre Auswanderung ohne Rücksicht auf
die Kosten durchzuführen. Sie scheuen dabei nicht vor unmittel-
barer oder mittelbarer Bestechung von Vertretern fremder
Staaten oder deren Gehilfen zurück. Sie sind bereit, für die
Erlangung eines Visums nach den von ihnen gewählten Ziel-
ländern beträchtliche Beträge zu opfern, die sehr oft 1ooo RM
bis 3ooo RM zusätzlich über den ordnungsgemäßen Gebühren lie-
gen. Die Reichsstelle hat zwar keine näheren Unterlagen dar-
über, in welchem Umfange solche Schmiergelder tatsächlich
gezahlt worden sind. Die Juden, die solche Schmiergelder
zahlen, geben hiervon nur selten Kenntnis. Bei der Reichsstelle herrscht die Auffassung, daß von den ausländischen
Vertretern der europäischen Staaten, der Vereinigten Staaten
von Nordamerika und der von den Briten beherrschten Länder
und Gebiete keine Schmiergelder der Juden angenommen wurden.
Anders ist es bei den Vertretern der mittel- und südameri-
kanischen Länder. Hier scheint bei manchen Vertretern die Erlangung eines Visums leicht und schnell erreichbar gewesen
zu sein, wenn über die Paßgebühren hinaus von den Juden oder
deren Beauftragten größere Zugelder geleistet wurden. Die
Reichsstelle ist der Auffassung, daß es im Interesse des
deutschen Ansehens mit allen Mitteln zu verhindern versucht
werden sollte, daß an Vertreter ausländischer Staaten mit
Amtssitz in Deutschland von den Juden oder deren Beauftragten
Schmiergelder geleistet werden, um diese Vertreter zu Hand-
lungen zu veranlassen, zu denen sie kraft ihres Amtes ver-

                                pflichtet

83-24

pflichtet sind. Insoweit Vertreter ausländischer Staaten im Auslande ihren Amtssitz haben und sich von den Juden oder deren
Beauftragten Schmiergelder zahlen lassen, besteht deutscherseits
dagegen kein besonderes Interesse, hiergegen vorstellig zu werden. Es ist Sache des Auslandes, über solche Vorkommnisse selbst
zu wachen.

In dem mitgeteilten Falle der Familie Leo Israel Zuckermann
bestand keine Notwendigkeit, über die ordnungsgemäßen Gebühren
hinaus noch für jedes Visum Schmiergelder an Vermittler in Höhe
von 2.500 RM pro Paß zu leisten. Der in Deutschland zugelassene
Konsul für Ecuador müßte in Deutschland angehalten werden können,
für einen Juden, der die gesetzlichen und sonst geforderten Ein-
reise- und Niederlassungserfordernisse erfüllt, ohne Schmiergelder
ein Visum gegen die üblichen Gebühren auszustellen. Bei der
Reichsvereinigung der Juden in Deutschland ist ermittelt worden,
ob Otto Israel Weißelberger von dort beauftragt war, Schmiergel-
dergeschäfte wie das der Familie Leo Israel Zuckermann zu vermit-
teln. Hierbei wurde festgestellt, daß Weißelberger diese Geschäf-
te auf eigene Rechnung gemacht hat. Da der Hilfsverein der Juden
auch sonst mit seiner Arbeit nicht zufrieden war, ist ihm gekün-
digt worden und er soll bereits seit einigen Wochen ausgewandert
sein.

Der Hauptfall, bei dem Juden Schmiergelder zu zahlen gezwun-
gen waren, ist folgender:

Die Juden, die bei ausländischen Konsulaten mit Amtssitz in
Deutschland, also bei ihren an sich zuständigen Konsulaten, ein
Visum nicht erhalten konnten, haben durch ihre Bekannten im Auslande (Freunde, Rechtsanwälte, gewerbsmäßige Vermittler) sehr oft
Mitteilungen erhalten, daß sie gegen bestimmte Leistungen in De-
visen, die sich in der Regel zwischen 100 - 300 Goldmark beweg-
ten, ordnungsgemäß ausgestellte Visa erhalten könnten. Es ist in
diesen Fällen natürlich nicht zu ermitteln gewesen, an wen diese
über die normalen Konsulargebühren hinaus gezahlten Gelder im
einzelnen gelangt sind. Als sicher ist jedoch anzunehmen, daß
auch fremden Konsuln und ihrem Personal ein Teil dieser Beträge
zugeflossen ist. Solange es sich hierbei um Schmiergelder handel-
te, die im Auslande an Ausländer gezahlt und die der Höhe nach
sich in mäßigen Grenzen hielten, hat die Reichsstelle für das
Auswanderungswesen hiergegen keine Bedenken gehabt, zumal da
in den meisten Fällen den Juden ihre ausländischen Freunde diese Schmiergelder bereitstellten. Solange es für auswanderungs-
willige

217

willige Juden möglich war, das gesperrte Vermögen an die Gold-
diskontbank zu verkaufen, war es auch unbedenklich, wenn die
Kosten für die Beschaffung von Visen im Auslande, durch Sperrmarkverkauf von den Juden aufgebracht wurden, die keine Bezie-
hungen im Auslande hatten oder hatten anknüpfen können. In diesen Fällen war die Freigabe durch die Devisenstelle nach unserer
Auffassung sehr erwünscht. Wenn aber die Juden zukünftig über
ihr Vermögen durch Sperrmarkverkauf nicht mehr verfügen können,
dann kommt eine Beschaffung eines Visums im Auslande für alle
Juden nur dann mehr in Frage, wenn sie von befreundeter Seite
im Auslande die Kosten für eine Visumbeschaffung schenkungs-
weise bereitgestellt erhalten. Zukünftig dürfte sich daher er-
übrigen, aus den gemäß § 59 Devisengesetz gesicherten Konten
Beträge für die Beschaffung von Visa im Auslande freizugeben.

gez. Schmidt

218

1939

13-24 30/9
~ 17/10
~ 17/11.
~ 2/12.
~ 28.12.

1940:
12.1.
19.1.
22.1.
3.2.
8.2.
6.3.
18.3.

21.5

2 688
3 498
5 197
6 051
6 052

Auswanderung von Juden
(über Italien)
nach Palästina

Berlin SW 11, den 17. Oktober 19 39
Prinz-Albrecht-Straße 8
Fernsprecher: 120040

An das

Auswärtige Amt

Berlin W 8,
Wilhelmstr. 72-76

220

Betrifft: Auswanderung von Juden über Italien.

Vorgang: Schreiben vom 5. 10. 39 - 83-24 30/9

    Da es nach wie vor erwünscht ist, wenn Juden
in möglichst grossem Umfange aus Deutschland auswandern,
bestehen auch diesseits keine Bedenken, Juden nach Italien
ausreisen zu lassen, selbst wenn sie erst dort das Einreisevisum für das eigentliche Zielland erlangen können.

    Dass Juden gegebenenfalls wieder nach Deutschland
zurückgenommen werden müssten, wenn sie im Einzelfall von
Italien aus nicht weiter könnten, muss m. E. mit in Kauf
genommen werden. Es bleibt dann immer noch vorbehalten ,
durch entsprechende innerdeutsche Maßnahmen die Juden zu
veranlassen, sich andere Auswanderungsmöglichkeiten zu
suchen.

    In Vertretung:

    gez. M ü l l e r .

Beglaubigt:

Kanzleiangestellte.

Berlin, den 25. Oktober 1939.

An

den Botschaftsrat der Königlih
Italienischen Botschaft
Herrn Gesandten Graf Magistrati

B e r l i n .

M.D.g.Pol. zu 83-24, 17/10.

U.St.S.R.Pol.

Note geprüft
und verschlossen
Bln. d. 25.10.

LR. Dr. Schumburg.

Sehr verehrter Graf Magistrati !

In Beantwortung Ihrer am 30.v.M. an
Herrn Unterstaatssekretär mündlich ge-
richteten Anfrage betreffend die Ver-
schiffung von etwa 1450 Juden über
Triest nach Palästina darf ich Ihnen auf
Grund der von den zuständigen deutschen
Behörden erteilten Auskunft folgendes
mitteilen:

1. Deutscherseits bestehen keine Bedenken, Juden deutscher Staatsangehörigkeit über Italien in ihre Ziel-
   länder ausreisen zu lassen, selbst
   wenn sie erst im italienischen Aus-
   reisehafen das Einreisevisum für ihr
   Zielland erhalten;

2. falls einzelne Juden in dem Ausreise-
   hafen Triest das Visum ihres Ziellandes
   nicht erhalten sollten, würde einer

Wieder-

Vor Abgang:

Pol. IV Italien

R-Pass

Nach Abgang:

Pol. II Engl.

Pol. V.

z.Kts.

221

Wiedereinreise dieser Juden in das Reichsgebiet seitens der zuständigen deutschen
Behörden keine Hindernisse in den Weg
gelegt werden.

Ich bleibe mit meinen verbindlichsten
Empfehlungen, sehr verehrter Graf Magistrati,

Ihr sehr ergebener

gez...........

222

Deutsche Botschaft
Rom

ROM, den 17.November 1939.

9083/39.

Betr: Ferenczy Sandor, Judentransporte nach Palästina.

Der in Berlin W.50, Schaperstr.6 wohnhafte Sandor
F e r e n c z y , seines Zeichens Automobilhändler, hat
hier vorgesprochen und mitgeteilt, er und ein gewisser
Alexander von Hoepfner seien im Einvernehmen mit dem
Hauptsicherheitsamt der Gestapo (Regierungsrat Lischka)
mit der Aufgabe betraut, Judentransporte aus dem Reich
nach Palästina zu organisieren. Zu diesem Zwecke hätte er
sich nach Griechenland und Italien begeben, um Schiffe zu
chartern. In Griechenland sei ihm der Ankauf von zwei
Schiffen gelungen. Gelder seien durch Sammlungen in ver-
schiedenen Ländern in genügendem Ausmasse vorhanden. Es
handle sich nun um die Frage, wie diese Transporte durch
Italien zu bringen seien, da die betreffenden Auswanderer
weder die Einwanderungserlaubnis nach Palästina noch den
Sichtvermerk des Ziellandes besässen.

223

Der Sachbearbeiter der Botschaft hat sich den
Mitteilungen gegenüber rezeptiv verhalten und darauf hin-
gewiesen, dass der Botschaft über die Aktion nichts bekannt sei und sie sich ohne Weisung mit der Angelegenheit
nicht befassen könne. Es wurde Herrn Ferenczy zur Frage
der Durchreise durch Italien lediglich gesagt, dass jüdische Auswanderer bei der Ein- oder Durchreise durch das
Land gewöhnlich den Nachweis zu erbringen hätten, dass
sie im Besitz der Einwanderungserlaubnis in ein bestimmtes
Land und der betreffenden Sichtvermerke seien.

An

das Auswärtige Amt

B e r l i n .

R'schr.l.b.-Durchschl. als Kont.

83-24 17/11.   N

bzf: 2 Dopp.des Eing.

Pol. IV   Abschriftlich   -doppelt-

z.K   der

Reichszentrale für jüdische Auswanderung
z.Hd.von Herrn Regierungsrat Lischka
- Geheimes Staatspolizeiamt -

zur Kenntnis und mit der Bitte um Äußerung übersandt, was

dort über die Angelegenheit bekannt ist.

Im Auftrag

gez.Schumburg

224

ab:

Der Chef der Sicherheitspolizei und des SD

S-IV (II Rz.) 651/39

Berlin SW 11, den 2. Dezember 1939
Prinz-Albrecht-Straße 8
Fernsprecher: 12 00 40

An das

Auswärtige Amt
z.Hd. Herrn Geheimrat Roediger

Berlin W 8

Wilhelmstr. 72-76

225

Betrifft: Auswanderung von Juden (Durchreise durch Italien)

Vorgang : Ohne

Anlagen : 1

Unter Bezugnahme auf die Vorsprache des Herrn Alexander von Höpfner aus Berlin bei Herrn Geheimrat Roediger am 30.11.39 überreiche ich in der Anlage Abschrift eines Berichtes des Herrn von Höpfner vom 1.12.39 über die von ihm geführten Verhandlungen in vorbezeichneter Angelegenheit. Ich teile hierzu und zwar gleichzeitig in Beantwortung des dortigen Schreibens vom 22.11.39 83-24 17/11 folgendes mit:

Herr Alexander von Höpfner steht in Angelegenheiten der Judenauswanderung als Inhaber eines Reisebüros in Berlin seit längerer Zeit mit mir in Verbindung. Er ist vor einiger Zeit mit meinem Einverständnis nach Griechenland und Italien gefahren, um dort weitere Möglichkeiten für eine Auswanderung von Juden, insbesondere unter den gegenwärtigen Verhältnissen zu erforschen. Da der Weg über Italien fast die einzige Möglichkeit ist, auf dem ~~die~~ Juden heute noch auswandern können, (auf den Hitler) ⌐

halt ich eine Klärung bei den zuständigen italienischen

Behörden zu der Frage des Durchreisesichtvermerks für vordringlich

und würde es begrüssen, wenn vor allem ein Durchreisesichtvermerk

seitens der italienischen Behörden auch dann erteilt wird,

wenn ein Einreisevisum des endgültigen Ziellandes noch

nicht vorliegt.

                    Im Auftrage:

                    [signature]

226

Abschrift

Alexander von Höpfner   Berlin N 15, 1.12.1939

S.S. Hauptsicherungsamt

II /B

z.Hd. d.Herrn Regierungsrat Lischka

Betrifft: Judenemigration nach Palästina.

        Infolge der Kriegsereignisse sind die bisher ab deutschen
Hafen geplanten Transporte zurzeit undurchführbar geworden. Die Transporte mit kleineren Schiffen über den Donauweg zu leiten, war
nur bis Einbruch des Winters möglich, es ist daher der einzig
noch verbleibende Weg einer Ausreise über Italien beschlossen worden,
und haben wir diesbezügliche Schritte derart unternommen, dass wir
mit neutralen Schiffsbesitzern zu einem Abkommen gelangt sind. Zurzeit
ist es möglich, einen unter panamäsischer Flagge fahrenden, 12000 tons
Passagierdampfer zu chartern, dessen Besitzer griechischer Staats-
angehöriger ist und auf unseren Wunsch zum Abschluss eines Vertrages
nach Venedig zu kommen bereit ist. Die Vorverhandlungen sind bis
zur Abschlussreife gediehen und ist auch eine Einschiffungsorganisation
in Venedig mit Hilfe der dortigen Firma Bassani bereits geschaffen.
Die notwendigen Passagegebühren in ausländischer Valuta sind ebenfalls
durchdie ausländischen Hilfsorganisationen der Juden gesichert.

        Als Abgangshafen ist Venedig als der am besten geeignete
gewählt worden, jedoch ist die Voraussetzung für ein ordnungsgemässes
An-bord-gehen der Emigranten die Erteilung eines Transitvisums seitens
der ital. Behörden. Deshalb ist in mündlicher Besprechung bereits
die Deutsche Botschaft in Rom (Legationsrat Dr.Strauss und Handels-
attaché Dr.Greff) informiert worden. Diese kann jedoch erst tätig
werden, wenn sie nochmals offiziell von ihrer Dienststelle, dem A.A.
in Berlin, hierzu aufgefordert wird. Es muss ausdrücklich bemerkt
werden, dass das Verlangen,welches an die ital.Behörde gerichtet wird,
sich- wenn irgend möglich- nicht nur auf die Erteilung von Visen für
eine einmalige Ausreise erstreckt,sondern auf eine prinzipielle
Genehmigung der Visen für laufende Transporte.

        Über das Vorstehende ist der Vorsitzende der Reichsvereinigung
der Juden in Deutschland, Dr. Eppstein, eingehend informiert und ist
mit dieser Lösung einverstanden.
                              Heil Hitler!
                              gez. v. Höpfner.

227

Berlin, den 16.Dezember 1939

zu 13-24 5/12

Zu R 40356

S o f o r t !

An

Diplogerma R o m

T e l e g r a m m
Geh. Chiffr. Verfahren

Telegramm Nr. 1042

Wie Botschaft durch Besprechungen
Höpfner mit Strauß und Greff bekannt,
sind größere Transporte von auswandern-
den deutschen Juden über Italien geplant.
Bitte bei dortiger Regierung sicherstellen,
daß Italien Durchreisesichtvermerke gegebenenfalls grundsätzlich erteilt und zwar
auch dann, wenn Einreisesichtvermerke
dritter Länder noch nicht vorliegen sollten.

Ref.: VLR.Rödiger

Zur Information: deutscherseits ist
gegenüber italienischen Anträgen auf
Durchreisesichtvermerke durch Deutschland für Reisende aus nordischen Ländern
einschließlich ausländischer Juden, die
auf italienischen Schiffen Passage belegt
haben, unter Zurückstellung erheblicher
Bedenken entgegenkommend zugesagt.
Drahtbericht.

228

Bei Pol I
Ref.Deutschland z.g.Mitz.

Nach Abgang: w.v.

Rödiger.

Albrecht.

415

Abgesandt 16.12.39 17

Telegramm eingeg. ROM 285   28/12 1945 =19   Uhr   Vor- Mitt.
                                                     Nach-

AUSWAERTIG BERLIN =

109028 AUF DRAHTERLASS 1042 VOM 16.12.   HIESIGES
AUSSENMINISTERIUM DAS AUCH VON ITALIENISCHER BOTSCHAFT IN
BERLIN IN GLEICHER SACHE BEFASST HAT SICH ZUNAECHST GENAUE
PRUEFUNG UNSERES WUNSCHES VORBEHALTEN, DA BEI
NICHTVORHANDENSEIN SICHTVERMERKS ZIELLANDES ANWACHSEN ANZAHL
HIER AUFHAELTLICHER JUDEN BEFUERCHTET WIRD. AUSSERDEM
HINWEIS DASS BEI ITALIENISCHEN ANTRAEGEN AUF DURCHREISE DURCH
DEUTSCHLAND FUER REISENDE AUS NORDISCHEN LAENDERN JUDEN
KEINESFALLS IN BETRACHT KAEMEN. WEITERER BERICHT VORBEHALTEN

                                        = PLESSEN +

229

Eingeg.: 28.12
Ch.:
Ch.:
Od.:
An Tel.-Komm.:   X

Berlin, dem // Dez. 1939.   zu 83-24 28/12.

An

das Reichssicherheitshauptamt

z.Hd.von Herrn RR.Lischka.

Auf das Schrb. v.2.d.M.
-S-IV (II Rz.) 651/39-
Betr. Auswanderung von Juden
(Durchreise durch Italien).

bei

Recht

Pol. I

z.Mitz.

230

Nach telegrafischem Bericht der Deutschen Botschaft in Rom hat sich das Italienische Außenministerium, das auch von der hiesigen Italienischen Botschaft mit der gleichen Angelegenheit befaßt worden ist, zunächst genaue Prüfung des vorgebrachten Wunsches vorbehalten, da offenbar die Befürchtung besteht, daß die Zahl der in Italien zurückbleibenden Juden anwächst, falls das Visum des Ziellandes nicht bereits bei der Einreise vorliegt. Gleichzeitig wurde seitens des Ital. Außenministeriums daraufhingewiesen, daß italienische Anträge auf Durchreise durch das Reichsgebiet lediglich nicht jüdische Reisende aus den nordischen Ländern beträfen.

Die Botschaft hat sich weiteren Bericht vorbehalten.

I.A.

ab: 6 ...   gez.Schunb rg

Der Chef der ~~Sicherheitspolizei~~ und des SD   Berlin, den 15. Januar 1940.
I V 8 Nr. 314 II/39 - 559 - gRs.

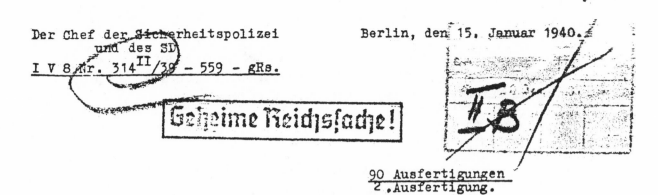

Geheime Reichssache!

90 Ausfertigungen
2.Ausfertigung.

An

a) das Amt IV (RZ)
h) alle Staatspolizei(leit)stellen

<u>nachrichtlich</u>

den Inspekteuren der Sicherheitspolizei und des SD
dem Befehlshaber der Sicherheitspolizei und des SD in Prag.

<u>Betrifft:</u> Jüdische Auswanderung.
<u>Bezug:</u>   Erlaß des Reichssicherheitshauptamtes vom 28.10.1939
           - I V 8 Nr. 265 III/39 - 559 - gRs.-

Doc. 14

231

- - -

     Auf Anordnung des Oberkommandos der Wehrmacht ist der Telefon-
und Telegrammverkehr nach dem nichtfeindlichen Ausland grundsätzlich gesperrt. Er kann nur von den Behörden, Firmen und Privatper-
sonen ausgeübt werden, die vom Oberkommando der Wehrmacht zugelassen
sind.

     Die beschleunigte Auswanderung von Juden macht in vielen Fällen
erforderlich, daß unmittelbar vor der Auswanderung zur Klärung ein-
zelner Fragen noch telegrafische Rückfragen bei den betreffenden
ausländischen Hilfsorganisationen gehalten werden (z.B. Rückfragen,
ob die Durchreisegenehmigung der Durchreisestaaten erteilt ist, Rückfrage zur Feststellung des erforderlichen Passagegeldes).

     Eine Aufgabe derartiger Telegramme durch die jüdischen Aus-
wanderer kann nicht zugelassen werden. Im Einvernehmen mit dem Ober-
kommand der Wehrmacht ordne ich daher an, daß die zuständigen
Staatspolizei(leit)stellen diese Telegramme nach dem nichtfeindlichen Ausland aufgeben. Die Zulassungsanträge sind von den jüdischen
Auswanderern an die Staatspolizei(leit)stellen zu richten.

                                    <u>Wegen</u>

Wegen der Überlastung der in Betrieb gebliebenen
Leitungen ist die Führung von Ferngesprächen nach dem
Ausland für den erwähnten Zweck nicht zulässig.

In Vertretung:
gez: Dr. B e s t.

Verw.-Sekretär.

232

Gro.

Abwehrstelle im Wehrkreis VI   Münster, d.1.2.40

Nr.119/40 III (N) g Kdos.

Bezug: Erlass des Chefs der Sicherheitspolizei und

       des S.D. von 15.1.1940

Betr.: Jüdische Auswanderung.

```
Staatspolizeistelle Aachen
                              6 Ausfertg.
E.K.            1. Ausfertg.
Eing.    6. Febr. 1940
Abteilung | Bearbeiter | Anlagen
```

        An die

           Staatspolizeistelle

                  Aachen

    Unter Bezug auf den o.a. Erlass des Chefs der Sicherheits-
polizei und des S.D. an die Staatspolizeistellen betr. jüdische
Auswanderung teilt Abwehrstelle mit, dass sie hier eingehende
Anträge von jüdischen Auswanderern auf Genehmigung zur Absen-
dung von Auslandstelegrammen der zuständigen Stapostelle mit
Stellungnahme zur Weitergabe übersenden wird.

    Abwehrstelle bittet, die dort eingehenden Zulassungsan-
träge jüdischer Auswanderer vor Absendung der Telegramme der
Abwehrstelle zwecks Stellungnahme ge. Vfg. O K W v.10.10.39
Nr.2428/39 g Kdos. Abw. III (N) zuzuleiten.

    Abwehrstelle wird dann wie in Absatz 1) verfahren.

233

        I.A.

TELEGRAM RECEIVED

CK   Berlin
This telegram must be
closely paraphrased be-**From**   Dated May 18, 1940
fore being communicated
to anyone. (Br)   Rec'd 3:30 p.m.

Secretary of State

   Washington

   1398, May 18, 1 p.m.

   My No. 1186, May 4, 9 a.m.

A member of the Embassy called recently by invitation

on Wohlthat who communicated the following information

regarding Jewish emigration from areas under German control

with the request that it be not made public.

   One. It is still Germany's policy to encourage emi-

gration of German, Austrian and Czech, Jews respectively

from the old Reich, Austria and the protectorate. He said

that the German authorities preferred to facilitate the

emigration of German, Austrian and Czech, Jews and hold

back the emigration of Polish or stateless Jews formerly

of Polish nationality from the three areas unless it could

be shown that the latter would not be charged to the German

Austrian, and Czech immigration quotas or otherwise retard

the emigration of German, Austrian and Czech Jews.

Wohlthat was orally informed that the place of birth

determined the quota to which immigrants were charged.

   (END OF SECTION ONE)

EMB   KIRK

TELEGRAM RECEIVED

Berlin

Dated May 18, 1940

Rec'd 4:46 p.m.

Secretary of State,

Washington.

1398, May 18, 1 p.m. (SECTION TWO)
                              had been
Two. While no formal order/issued prohibiting

the immigration of Jews from Polish districts now in-

corporated into Germany or from the General Government

of Poland the Ministry of Interior was as a general

practice at the present time refusing to allow Jewish

departures from those areas in the belief that any

considerable movement from those regions might retard

Jewish emigration from the old Reich, Austria and

the protectorate. In this connection it has been the

observation of the consular section of the Embassy

that the German restrictions on the immigration of

Jews of Polish nationality and stateless Jews formerly

Polish nationals do not extend to Polish born state-

less Jews who possess German nationality. The latter

apparently receive German passports without undue diffi-

culties and are obtaining American visas fairly rapidly

as their turn on the visa waiting list is advanced

because of the inability of non-German Polish born

stateless Jews enjoying prior registration on the list

to

235

-2- #1392, May 18, 1 p.m., from Berlin.

to obtain travel documents with which to appear for
visa examinations.

Three. Wohlthat indicated, however, that if the
German authorities could be convinced that the emigration of Polish Jews would not tend to absorb the number
of Jewish immigrants which foreign countries were
willing to receive and thereby retard the emigration
of German, Austrian and Czech Jews the German Government might reconsider and permit Jewish departures
from the annexed provinces and eventually the General
Government. In such case, however, the authorities
would prefer that Polish Jews in the annexed provinces
should emigrate in advance of those in the General
Government.

                                        KIRK

EMB

TELEGRAM RECEIVED

RDS
This telegram must be
closely paraphrased be-
fore being communicated FROM
to anyone. (br.)

Berlin

Dated May 18, 1940

Rec'd 6 p.m.

Secretary of State,

    Washington.

    1398, May 18, 1 p.m. (SECTION THREE)

    Four. He stated that according to his information
there were in General/ Government Poland some 1,269,000 Jews
and 632,000 in annexed regions. The question of the
transfer of a part of the Jews from the latter districts to General/ Government Poland was receiving consideration but no decision had been reached nor would he
thought any action be taken until after the war. He
remarked that it would of course be impracticable to
transfer all the 632,000 Jews in the Polish provinces
now incorporated in Germany to the General/ Government areas.

    Five. According to German statistics some 10,300
Jews emigrated from the old Reich, Austria and the
protectorate during the first three months of 1940 of
which 4,500 went to North America, 2,400 to central
and South America, 400 to Palestine, 1700 to Asia and
1200 to European countries and the balance to Africa
and Australasia. The total was almost exactly divided
between males and females. Of the total some 1500 were

                     eighteen

237

-2- #1398, May 18, 1 p.m., from Berlin.

eighteen years.of age or less some 4400 aged between
eighteen and fortyfive, 2700 between fortyfive and
sixty years and 1650 over sixty years of age. In
April Jewish emigration from these three sections of
greater Germany totalled 4133 mainly to North America.
Figures for emigration from September 1 to December 31
were lacking.

                                        KIRK

EMB

238

TELEGRAM RECEIVED

CK   **FROM**   Berlin
This telegram must be
closely paraphrased be-   Dated May 18, 1940
fore being communicated
to anyone. (Br)   Rec'd 4:08 p.m.

Secretary of State

    Washington

    1398, May 18, 1 p.m. (SECTION FOUR)

    It was not thought advisable without direction from
the Department to discuss the indirect request set forth
in paragraph three above nor to point out to Wohlthat
that it would not (repeat not) be possible under our
immigration laws and regulations to assign the whole or
any part of the Polish quota for the use of Jewish residents   **239**
of the districts formally annexed to Germany. Practically
of course by refusing to grant passports or exit visas t
Jews in General Government Poland the German Government
might endeavor to insure that relatively a larger part
of the Polish quota be made available for the emigration
of Jews from the new German eastern provinces.

    It might be inferred from Wohlthat's statements that
it is the present intention of the Reich to maintain the
General Government in some form of separate status.

    (END OF MESSAGE)

                                              KIRK

EMB

1940:   9. 4.
913

Leo Israel Fischer

83-24

241

Berlin, den 13 6. 1940. I.D. III 83- 9/4

fg. ~~Doppel~~ des Eingangs

Ref.: L.R. ~~Schumburg~~ Rademacher

vor Abgang

Pol. IX

Recht

Kultur

N.P.

zur Mitz.

zur Kenntn

Termin

nach Wochen n.F.

Vm.

[handschriftlicher Vermerk]

Rtp. 25/40

ab: 14/6

Abschriftlich

nebst ~~Anlagen~~

~~- diese unter Rückerbittung -~~

dem

~~Reichsminister des Innern~~
~~Reichsminister für Volksauf-
klärung und Propaganda~~
Reichsführer SS und Chef der
Deutschen Polizei im Reichs-
ministerium des Innern
~~Reichssicherheitshauptamt~~

~~je besonders (Sammelanschrift)~~

~~auf das Schreiben vom~~

~~im Anschluß an das Schreiben vom~~

zur Kenntnis

I.A.

gez. ~~Schumburg~~
Rademacher

**Der Chef der Sicherheitspolizei
und des SD**

— IV D 4 —   7735/40 —

Bitte in der Antwort vorstehendes Geschäftszeichen u. Datum anzugeben

Berlin SW 11, den _18. Juli_ 19⁴⁰.
Prinz-Albrecht-Straße 8
Fernsprecher: 12 00 40

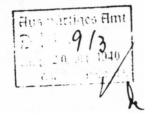

An das

Auswärtige Amt,
z.Hd. Herrn Legationssekretär Rademacher,

B e r l i n .

243

<u>Betrifft:</u> Umzugsgut des Juden Leo Israel Fischer,
geb. 19.11.1902, derzeitiger Aufenthalt
Bolivien.

<u>Vorgang</u> : Dortiges Schreiben vom 13.6.1940
B.Nr. D III 83-24 9./4.

Die Ermittlungen in obenstehender Angelegenheit haben ergeben, dass Leo Israel Fischer,
der am 27. August 1937 von Wien nach Bolivien
ausgewandert ist, ständig an verschiedene in-
und ausländische Komitees und Behörden Eingaben
in den verschiedensten Angelegenheiten richtet.

Die Israelitische Kultusgemeinde Wien,
der die Angelegenheit bekannt ist, bezeichnet
Fischer als unzurechnungsfähig. Sie ist bereits
an jüdische Komitees im Ausland herangetreten,
um die umfangreichen und unbegründeten Gesuche
des Genannten zu unterbinden.

Die im Gesuch angeführten Gegenstände
des Fischer existieren zum Teil überhaupt nicht
und soweit welche vorhanden sind, handelt es
sich um wertlose Sachen, deren Verbringung nach

83-24 .   ./.

Übersee in keinem Verhältnis zu den Transportkosten stehen würden.

Bezüglich Beschaffung eines Führungszeugnisses wurde der Antragsteller seitens der Israelitischen Kultusgemeinde Wien wiederholt, bisher erfolglos aufgefordert, die entsprechenden Unterlagen einzusenden.

Im Auftrage:

[Unterschrift: Eichmann]

244

Vermerk.

Da der Jude Fischer als Querulant bezeichnet werden kann, ist von einer Beantwortung seiner Eingabe abzusehen.

Vfg.

Zu den Akten.

Berlin, den 25. Juli 1940.

OFFICE OF CHIEF OF COUNSEL
FOR WAR CRIMES
APO 696 - A   US ARMY

<u>STAFF EVIDENCE ANALYSIS, MINISTRIES DIVISION</u>

By: Betty D. Richardson
Date: 1 October 1947

Document number: NG - 3104

Title and/or general nature: Letter from SCHELLENBERG
with distribution as below
with regard to Jewish
emigration from France and
Belgium. In view of the
coming "radical solution",
this is to be stopped.

Form of Document.   Mimeographed copy.
Stamp of D III. Secret.
Note by RADEMACHER forwarding
the letter to: 1) Dr. LOCHNER ??
2) Pg? AUFRICHTER ?? 3)Sofort
SCHELLENBERG in Rueckschluss.
Unrecognizable initials show
acknowledgement of receipt,

Doc. 17

Date: 20 May 1941

245

Source: D IIIg 1941 151-512
Inl. ... ./. D 498048
now at Mc Nair, Barracks
Berlin, BC-SD Mission, Bldg "
Photostatic copy deposited at
Documents Room, OCC C,Nuernberg.
OCC BLT 4816

PERSONS OR ORGANIZATIONS IMPLICATED:
RADEMACHER   Distribution to
LOCHNER ??   all Stapo
AUFRICHTER ??   Offices
SCHELLENBERG   Commissioner of
the Chief of
SD Sections)   Sip and SD for
D III of the)   France
Foreign)   SPANAGEL
Office)

TO BE FILED UNDER THESE REFERENCE HEADINGS.
NG - Foreign Office
NG - Racial and Political
Persecution
NOSS

SUMMARY.
SCHELLENBERG says that German Jews in France and
Belgium have been asking various authorities in the Reich
for their papers so as to enable them to emigrate.
- 1 -

While existing policy provides for the encouragement of
migration, travel facilities are very limited and for this
reason, "and because of the final solution of the Jewish
question which is surely approaching, the emigration of Jews
from France and Belgium is to be stopped."

While each individual case is to be considered on
merits, the general rule will now be that emigration must
be stopped.

(Analyst's note: the additional filing references at the
        end of the letter are being investigated.)

246

END

Reichssicherheitshauptamt   Berlin, den 2o. Mai 1941
IV B 4b (Rz)(neu) 2494/41 g
          (250)
_____

                    Geheim

    1) An
       alle Staatspolizei(leit)stellen

    2) den
       Beauftragten des Chefs der Sicherheitspolizei
       und des SD für Belgien und Frankreich
       über den Militärbefehlshaber in Frankreich
       General von Stülpnagel - persönlich -

    3) Nachrichtlich
       der SD-(Leit)Abschnitten   247

    4) dem
       Auswärtigen Amt - Abteilung D III -

    Betrifft: Auswanderung von Juden aus Belgien,
              dem besetzten und unbesetzten Frank-
              reich - Auswanderung von Juden aus
              dem Reichsgebiet in das unbesetzte
              Frankreich.

    Bezug: Ohne.

         Juden deutscher Staatsangehörigkeit,
    die sich z.Zt. in Frankreich und Belgien auf-
    halten, suchen bei verschiedenen Behörden im
    Reichsgebiet um Nachsendung von Urkunden, z.B.
    Reisepässe, Nährungszeugnisse usw., zum Zwecke
    der Auswanderung an.

         Gemäß einer Mitteilung des Reichs-
    marschalls des Großdeutschen Reiches ist die

Judenauswanderung aus dem Reichsgebiet einschliesslich Protektorat Böhmen und Mähren auch während des Krieges verstärkt im Rahmen der gegebenen Möglichkeiten unter Beachtung der aufgestellten Richtlinien für die Judenauswanderung durchzuführen. Da für die Juden aus dem Reichsgebiet z.Zt. nur ungenügend Ausreisemöglichkeiten, in der Hauptsache über Spanien und Portugal, vorhanden sind, würde eine Auswanderung von Juden aus Frankreich und Belgien eine erneute Schmälerung derselben bedeuten. Unter Berücksichtigung dieser Tatsachen und im Hinblick auf die zweifellos kommende Endlösung der Judenfrage ist daher die Auswanderung von Juden aus Frankreich und Belgien zu verhindern.

Ich bitte, die in Frage kommenden innerdeutschen Behörden des dortigen Dienstbereiches zu unterrichten, dass eine Nachsendung von Urkunden an Juden in Frankreich und Belgien zum Zwecke der Auswanderung nicht erfolgen soll.

Bezüglich der Auswanderung von Juden aus dem Reichsgebiet einschliesslich Protektorat Böhmen und Mähren in das unbesetzte Frankreich teile ich mit, dass im allgemeinen in besonders gelagerten Fällen, z.B. Übersiedlung mittelloser Juden zu Verwandten im unbesetzten Frankreich, falls kein sicherheitspolizelliches Interesse an einer Verhinderung der Auswanderung besteht, nach Vorliegen der Einwanderungsbewilligung der französischen Regierung der Auswanderung stattgegeben werden kann. Massgebend hierbei ist die Feststellung, dass durch die Genehmigung der Auswanderung von Juden in das unbesetzte Frankreich ein Vorteil des Deutschen Reiches entsteht, und sei es

248

auch nur durch die Tatsache, dass ein Jude das
Reichsgebiet verlässt.

Sollte es sich in Einzelfällen zeigen,
dass die Einwanderungsbewilligung seitens der
französischen Regierung nur im Hinblick auf ge-
wisse Vorteile, die Frankreich durch die Einwanderung dieser Juden entstehen würden, erteilt
wurde, so ist in diesen Fällen die Auswanderungs-
genehmigung zu versagen. In jedem Einzelfall
ist jedoch die vorherige Stellungnahme des Reichs-
sicherheitshauptamtes einzuholen.

Eine Einwanderung von Juden aus den
übrigen europäischen Ländern in das unbesetzte
Frankreich ist nicht erwünscht, wenngleich diese
nicht immer verhindert werden kann.

Eine Einwanderung von Juden in die von
uns besetzten Gebiete ist im Hinblick auf die
zweifellos kommende Endlösung der Judenfrage zu
verhindern.

249

Zusatz für den Beauftragten des Chefs der
Sicherheitspolizei und des SD für Belgien
und Frankreich.

Zu dem Schreiben der Dienststelle Paris vom
29.4.1941 - II 5 2 SA 234 -

Zu dem FS der Dienststelle Brüssel vom 9.5.1941
- II C -

- 4 -

NG - 3104

Zusatz für Einsatzkommando Paris

Zu dem FS vom 25.4.1941 Nr. 7664.

Zusatz für Staatspolizeileitstelle Karlsruhe

Zu dem FS vom 28.2.1941 - IV D 4 - 2 (Rz) -
299/41 -

Zusatz für das Auswärtige Amt, Abtlg. D III

Zu dem Schreiben vom 21.4.1941 - D III 3151 -
Zu dem Schnellbrief vom 28.4.1941 - D III 3426 -
Zu dem Schreiben vom 14.5.1941 - D III 3785 -

250

In Vertretung:
gez. S c h e l l e n b e r g

Beglaubigt:
Kanzleiangestellte.

STAFF EVIDENCE ANALYSIS, Ministries Division

                              By: Betty D. Richards
                              Date: 1 October 1947

Document Number: NG - 3107

Title and/or general nature: Correspondence between RADEMACHE
                              LUTHER, WEIZSÄCKER, and the Swe
                              Embassy showing how the Foreign
                              Office (particularly ALBRECHT and
                              WEIZSAECKER) continually refused
                              without any reason given, to sen
                              the necessary papers for the emi
                              tion of German Jews, originally
                              scheduled to leave for Madagasca
                              and now stranded in unoccupied
                              France (See BBT 4821)

Form of Document: A) Original typescript;
                              B) "   "

Stamps and other endorsements: A) Initialled LUTHER 18/9. Ink
                                  note "and VLR ALBRECHT - R .
                              B) Secret Initialled RADEMACHE
                                  and LUTHER, and HILGER??

Date: A) 15 September 1941;
                              B) 19 September 1941.

Source: D IIIg 1941 151-512 Inl.IIg.7/2
                              D 498048. Photostatic copy depos
                              ted at Documents Room, OCCWC, Nu
                              berg.

                              now at: McNair Barracks, Berlin
                                      FO-SD Mission Building
                                      OCC - BBT 4813 A,B.

PERSONS OR ORGANIZATIONS IMPLICATED:

                              LUTHER
                              ALBRECHT
                              RADEMACHER
                              WEIZSAECKER

TO BE FILED UNDER THESE REFERENCE HEADINGS:

                              NG - Foreign Office
                              NG - Racial and Political Persec

Doc. 18

251

- 1 -   over

STAFF EVIDENCE ANALYSIS, Ministries Division NG - 3107

SUMMARY:

A) Letter from RADEMACHER to WEIZSAECKER and ALBRECH'
via LUTHER, requesting instructions, RADEMACHER says that for
some time the Swedish Embassy has been asking for birth, marr;
ge etc. papers to be sent for the German Jews interned in un-
occupied France, so that they may continue their journey abroa

The Chief of the Sipo and SD, and the Ministry of
the Interior, however, no longer wish the emigration to take
place, and the German Embassy in Paris has been informed that
no further papers are to be provided.

RADEMACHER submits the draft of a note to the
Swedish Embassy, requesting it, but without giving any reason
to refrain from accepting further Jewish requests for papers.

B) Letter from RADEMACHER to LUTHER saying he has co
sulted ALBRECHT on the matter, who has suggested that nothing
definite should be said at the moment, but a policy of delay
pursued.

252

Referat D III   zu D III 7276

Verfügung vom 15.9.1941
zunächst nicht aus-   A u f z e i c h n u n g
führen.   ─────────────────────

Siehe Aufzeichnung
zu D III 440.5   Auf Veranlassung der Königlich Schwedischen
                           Gesandtschaft in Frankreich als Vertreterin der dor-
                           tigen deutschen Interessen bittet die hiesige König-
                           lich Schwedische Gesandtschaft seit einiger Zeit in
                           zahlreichen Verbalnoten um die Beschaffung und Über-
                           sendung von Pässen, polizeilichen Führungszeugnissen,
                           Geburts-, Heirats- und Sterbeurkunden und ähnlichen
                           Ausweispapieren für die im unbesetzten Frankreich inter-
                           nierten deutschen J u d e n . Diese Papiere sollen
                           augenscheinlich zur Weiterwanderung nach Übersee
                           dienen.
                               Im Einvernehmen mit dem Reichsministerium des Innern
                           und dem Chef der Sicherheitspolizei und des SD
                           (D III 774, 3151, 6804 und 7228) wird aber diese   253
                           Weiterwanderung als unerwünscht angesehen, da dadurch
                           die ohnedies geringen Passagemöglichkeiten für Juden
                           aus dem Reichsgebiet einschließlich des Protektorats
                           Böhmen und Mähren eine erneute Schmälerung erfahren
                           würden. Die gleichen Bedenken bestehen hinsichtlich
                           der Ausnutzung der überseeischen Einwanderungsquoten.
                               Der Deutschen Botschaft Paris -Konsularabteilung-
                           ist auf ihren diesbezüglichen Bericht vom 10. April 1941
                           - K 3815/DR 3 Nr.2/4C - am 21. April 1941 unter D III
                           3151 mitgeteilt worden, daß die Übersendung von Pässen,
                           Heimatscheinen, polizeilichen Führungszeugnissen und
                           ähnlichen Ausweispapieren zum Zwecke der Erleichterung
                           der Auswanderung von Juden seitens der inneren Behörden
                           eingestellt werden soll. Soweit die Juden sich mit
                           ihren Anliegen an das Deutsche Rote Kreuz gewandt haben
                           (D III 1975/41), ist dieses unter dem 8. September 1941
                                                                     - D III

                                      JJ 4156

- D III 7084 - im gleichen Sinne verständigt worden.

D III beabsichtigt mit nebenstehender Verbalnote nunmehr auch die Königlich Schwedische Gesandtschaft in Berlin ohne Angabe von Gründen zu bitten,
die Königlich Schwedische Gesandtschaft in Frankreich als Vertreterin der dortigen deutschen Interes-
sen zur sofortigen Einstellung der Annahme von Gesu-
chen dort wohnender deutscher Juden auf Besorgung
von Personalpapieren zu veranlassen.

Von der Rechtsabteilung (R VI a) sind bisher
etwa 350 Urkunden gebührenpflichtig beschafft und
weitergeleitet worden.

Hiermit
über Herrn Unterstaatssekretär Luther
Herrn Staatssekretär von Weizsäcker

mit der Bitte um Weisung vorgelegt.

Berlin, den 15. September 1941.

254

Berlin, den   September 1941   zu D III 7276

1. An

    die Königlich Schwedische Gesandtschaft
          - Abteilung B -

          B e r l i n

U.   St.S.

V e r b a l n o t e

Ref.: LR Rademacher

    Das Auswärtige Amt beehrt sich, der
tit. Gesandtschaft auf die Verbalnote vom
12. Juli 1941 - V 203 - und im Anschluß an
seine Verbalnote vom 17. Juli 1941 -R 59190-
mitzuteilen, daß die Ausstellung und Übersendung von Leumundszeugnissen für:

1. Albert Kaufmann, geb. am 4.6.1907
                 in Heidelberg-Handschuhs-
                 heim

2. Vor Abgang:

    Pol II

    R VI a

    mit der Bitte um
    Kenntnisnahme vorge-
    legt.

2. Ludwig Kaufmann, geb. am 24.3.1911 in
                 in Heidelberg-Handschuh-
                 heim,

3. Gerda Kaufmann geborene Fleischhacker,
           geb. am 9.11.1913 in
           Hochenheim (Baden)

255

aus grundsätzlichen Erwägungen nicht erfolgen kann.

    Das Auswärtige Amt bittet, der Königlich
Schwedischen Gesandtschaft in Frankreich als
Vertretung der dortigen deutschen Interes-
sen von der Ablehnung Kenntnis zu geben und
ihr nahezulegen, künftig Gesuche dort wohn-
hafter deutscher Juden auf Übersendung von
Pässen, Personenstandsurkunden und anderer
Personalpapiere nicht mehr entgegenzunehmen.

        Berlin, den   September 1941.

         (i.A.o.U.)

3. Nach Abgang wiedervorzulegen
    wegen Ablehnung der D III noch
    vorliegenden gleichartigen Noten
    (D III 6206, 6863, 7485-87)
    unter Bezugnahme auf obige Note.

Ref.: LR Rademacher

D III 440. 8

Wiedervorgelegt am:
5. MÄRZ 1942

Wiedervorgelegt am:
29. Nov. 1941

256

A u f z e i c h n u n g .

Weisungsgemäß habe ich mich wegen der Frage der
Schwedischen Gesandtschaft in Frankreich als Deutsche
Schutzmacht an Herrn VLR Albrecht gewandt und ihm
gleichzeitig den Fall über die von den Schweden erbetene
Erteilung von Leumundszeugnissen für die Juden deutscher
Staatsangehörigkeit in Frankreich dargelegt. Herr
VLR Albrecht schlug vor, die Sache zur Zeit nicht zur
Entscheidung zu bringen, sondern dilatorisch zu be-
handeln. Man solle sie auf 4 Wochen Frist legen, in-
zwischen würden voraussichtlich in ganz Frankreich
Deutsche Konsulate eingerichtet sein. Jedenfalls habe
ein entsprechender Vortrag Botschafter Abetz' beim
Führer dessen Billigung gefunden. Dadurch würde sich der
Schutzmacht-Auftrag der Schweden in Frankreich und
der Nordamerikaner in Deutschland erledigen. Den
Schweden könnte dann in einer Note mitgeteilt werden,
die Sache würde als gegenstandslos betrachtet, nachdem
der Schutzmachtvertrag erloschen sei.

Hiermit

Herrn Unterstaatssekretär L u t h e r
mit der Bitte um Weisung vorgelegt, ob dem Vorschlage
des Herrn VLR Albrecht gemäß vorgegangen werden soll.

Berlin, den 19. September 1941

2 1 Okt. 1941